WE KNOW IN PART

WE KNOW
IN PART

by

D. T. Niles

THE WESTMINSTER PRESS
Philadelphia

LIBRARY OF CONGRESS CATALOG CARD No. 64–18685

PUBLISHED BY THE WESTMINSTER PRESS®
PHILADELPHIA, PENNSYLVANIA

PRINTED IN THE UNITED STATES OF AMERICA

To
the memory of
JOHN BAILLIE

Contents

Preface

THIS BOOK AROSE out of my reactions to *Honest to God,* by John A. T. Robinson, Bishop of Woolwich (The Westminster Press, Philadelphia, and SCM Press, Ltd., London, 1963). When I had finished writing it, I gave it to one of my missionary friends in Ceylon who had been in England when *Honest to God* was published there, and who knew something of the immense help which that book gave to many who had found themselves unable to understand or accept the Christian faith as it was addressed to them. He also had shared with me, in conversation, some of the perplexities which that book had raised in his own mind as well as in the minds of many Christians.

When my friend returned the manuscript to me, he also sent me the following note: "In the minds of many of Robinson's 'atheist' readers, there is a feeling that the Biblical categories are themselves outmoded, and that what needs to be demonstrated is, not whether Robinson is true to the Bible, but whether the Bible itself is comprehensible and acceptable to adult man. I can think of a number of readers who, reading your book, would say, 'O.K., Robinson and the Bible are not in agreement, but we prefer Robinson'—and to them it doesn't seem you proffer any real help. You have addressed yourself (perhaps consciously) to the perplexed Christian, and in do-

9

ing so you have certainly given him much help and understanding. The other task still needs to be done."

This is fair comment. In large measure what Bishop Robinson's book will do in Asia and Africa is to perplex the Christian: and it is not unlikely that I have had them very much in mind as I wrote my book. I also have had in mind Bishop Robinson's own claim that, in his book, he was setting forward the substance of the Christian faith in a more adequate terminology and in more acceptable ways of thought than that of the Bible. I have been driven to the conclusion that the Bishop cannot substantiate that claim.

But the problem to which the Bishop addresses himself still remains, and about it something has to be said. I would say, first of all, that the true standpoint from which Bishop Robinson's own book must be judged is its success in winning a hearing for the Christian proclamation rather than its success in stating the Christian faith. When those who normally will not listen have been helped to listen, a great deal has been done. It is essential to keep them listening. But, if this listening is to issue in faith in God in Jesus Christ, then a great deal more needs to be done. Three things in particular are necessary. First, it is necessary that the world be affirmed.

The world [says Ronald Gregor Smith] is very suspicious, and rightly so, of those who cry "The temple of the Lord are these," for it has had long experience of the unbridled ambitions of the Church over against the world. What the world would really see gladly is an honest and complete recognition, without any ulterior motives, by those who claim to carry forward the message of Christianity, of the existence of the world with all its own principles of movement, hopes and possibilities.[1]

[1] Ronald Gregor Smith, *The New Man: Christianity and Man's Coming of Age* (Harper & Row, Publishers, Inc., 1956; SCM Press, Ltd., London, 1956), pp. 68 f.

Secondly, it is necessary, that the church earn its right to speak. In the words of Dietrich Bonhoeffer:

> Our Christianity today will be confined to praying for and doing right by our fellow men. Christian thinking, speaking and organization must be reborn out of this praying and this action . . . but the day will come when men will be called again to utter the word of God with such power as will change and renew the world. . . . Until then the Christian cause will be a silent and hidden affair, but there will be those who pray and do right and wait for God's own time.[2]

A. R. Vidler comments:

> Christians should restrain their spate of words, their pious and theological jargon, and keep quiet until they have proved in their commerce with the life of the world which of their words ring true.[3]

And thirdly, it is necessary for a new formulation of the faith

> to go back to the original foundations, resting it once more upon faith's primary insight rather than upon the dogmas that were so long ago formulated for the preservation of that insight.[4]

To put it simply, the immediate challenge is that the accent in Christian obedience must fall more heavily and

[2] Dietrich Bonhoeffer, *Letters and Papers from Prison* (SCM Press, Ltd., London, 1953), pp. 140–141. Published by The Macmillan Company in 1954, under the title *Prisoner for God*. Reprinted with permission of The Macmillan Company. Copyright 1953 by The Macmillan Company.

[3] The essay "Religion and the National Church" in *Soundings*, ed. by A. R. Vidler (Cambridge University Press, Cambridge, 1962), p. 247.

[4] John Baillie, *The Sense of the Presence of God* (Charles Scribner's Sons, 1962; Oxford University Press, London, 1962), p. 165. Reprinted with permission of Charles Scribner's Sons (Copyright © 1962 F. Jewel Baillie), and Oxford University Press.

more consistently than it has done before on the word of
Jesus that his disciples be "in the world" (John 17:11,
15). When this is done, and only then, will the listening of men be charged with expectancy as they hear the
message of God for them in Jesus Christ.

And, when they do listen, they must hear, not a muffled note, not an uncertain sound, not some improvised
harmony which happens to be the immediate fashion,
but that Living Word which calls to repentance, an-
nounces forgiveness, and leads to discipleship.

In this task, criticism of one another, as together we
seek to communicate Him who, in the final accounting,
must communicate Himself, is itself part of the attempt
at communication. The kind of book or books that my
missionary friend calls for can be written in the West
only by those who truly belong there and understand it
as part of themselves. Similar books will have to be written for every continent and culture. The whole enterprise, however, is one, and there is mutual support in
every effort; nor in this enterprise, must a premium be
put on those books which are demonstrably orthodox. If
to find the Christian faith is not so much to accept a
body of teaching as to find Christ and be found of him,
then orthodoxy itself becomes part of the gift of Christ:
so that the prolegomena of evangelism have their own
validity.

The hopes and burdens of Christian controversy are
always held within the ministry of the Christ himself
who makes himself known as we converse with one another on the way (Luke 24:17).

                                          D. T. Niles

Mercymere
Valalai, Atchuvely, Ceylon

Introduction

THIS BOOK HAS BEEN CONCEIVED as a sequel to
Honest to God. It is a sequel and not a reply, because,
in his own words, what the Bishop of Woolwich is seeking to do is "to help those who are on the fringes of the
Faith or quite outside it." The intention of his book, the
Bishop has said, "is a missionary one. This concern determines almost every line of what I wrote."[1] That which is
attempted in this sequel is to draw out the implications
and note the direction of the arguments in the Bishop's
book. One thing is clear, and that is that the Bishop has
succeeded in making Christian thought provocative in
the West and in guiding back to Christian ways of
thought many for whom the Christian faith and its wisdom had lost all significance.

A persistent question that, throughout the reading of
the Bishop's book and in the writing of this sequel, I
have felt compelled to keep in the foreground is the question about Jesus Christ. There are many questions that
men do ask concerning God and that must be taken
seriously in any religious discussion. But, in the last analysis, the missionary intention is fulfilled only when the
question that God has asked of men in Jesus Christ is
pressed home. The issue is not whether our understand-

[1] From a press report, quoted in *Ecumenical Press Service*,
May 17, 1963.

ing of God is illumined for us by the person, teaching,
and work of Jesus Christ; nor whether in him is found a
supreme illustration of God-consciousness; but whether
our faith in God is such as to find its one possibility in
him. Thirty years ago, when I was a student at the Theological College in Bangalore, Rev. Mark Sanjiva Rao, a
convert from Hinduism, gave us a series of lectures on
"Types of Religious Consciousness—Hindu and Christian."[2] These lectures left an indelible mark on my mind:
they taught me once and for all the real nature both of
the judgment and the promise that lie in the words of
Jesus: "No one comes to the Father, but by me" (John
14:6). It is not enough to say, "I believe in God." Any
African or Asian can tell what an intolerable burden
many forms of this belief are; while, in the West, it is
the general absence of this belief which is the burden.
The Western intellectual who finds it difficult to believe
in God shows every sign of being preoccupied by his
unbelief.

No, Jesus Christ does not represent an addition to
man's religious possibility, nor is it enough simply to explain, in terms of Jesus Christ, the inescapability of God
in human life. It is necessary, and this is what is involved in the missionary intention, to seek to lead men to
their encounter with Jesus Christ, so that, in his presence,
they may answer the questions he asks of them concerning their life, their destiny, and their discipleship.

Bishop Robinson's book proves, if proof were necessary,
that should we attempt to speak about God directly, it is
hardly possible to find our way through the intellectual
twists and turnings that such a discussion involves. The
argument concerning the nature of God's transcendence
and its relation to human existence is an unending argument. But let a man meet Jesus, and he will find that in

[2] Published by the Basel Mission Book and Tract Depository,
Bangalore, India.

that meeting is the true beginning of the argument about God; the essence of the answer, too, is provided in that meeting, for here is the "other." It may be impermissible to speak about God as a person alongside other persons, it is impossible to speak about Jesus Christ in any other way. The consequence of the incarnation is to set men irrevocably and unmistakably before God to be addressed and to answer.

Indeed, is not the "news" this: that the God whom we cannot see becomes the man whom we do see; that, without question, the relationship is established between God and man as I to Thou; and that each man finds his own questions overruled by God's double question addressed to him: Where are you? and, Where is your brother? Man must reveal both his hiding place and his burying place: he must account to God both for himself and for his brother, Jesus.

There are three challenges to the mold in which statements of the Christian faith are commonly cast, challenges that the Bishop contends must be met. There is the challenge of the scientific way of thought which demands the abrogation of the supranatural. There is the challenge of historical thinking which asks that the transhistorical meaning of events be expressed in nonmythological language. There is also the challenge of men without religion who ask whether the Christian faith is simply to fill the gaps in human knowledge and strengthen the sinews of men when they are weak, or whether it can be faith for "man come of age"[3] who has already found for himself a faith in the high purpose of human destiny.[4]

[3] This phrase "man come of age" is a phrase used by Bonhoeffer. Commenting on it, Bishop Robinson says: "For the educated minority this 'coming of age' does indeed imply an intellectual maturity, but in most merely a psychological stage of development in which religion and its attempt to keep man in strings is dismissed as childish. But it is none the less real for that." (*Honest to God,* p. 104. Hereafter abbreviated HG.) It

What the Bishop has sought to do is to set out, first of all, Paul Tillich's answer to the first challenge. He finds in the concept of self-transcendence an adequate way of stating the Christian faith within ontological categories. I have felt compelled to ask whether this is truly so. It has seemed to me that the concept of self-transcendence will just not do to express what is really meant by the grace of God as it is known and declared in the Christian faith, nor will it do to explain the true significance of "miracle" as it is experienced in the Christian life and as it was evidenced in the life of Jesus Christ.

Secondly, the Bishop feels that Rudolf Bultmann is right in the way in which he formulates and answers the challenge to demythologize. Bultmann's answer to the problem is essentially to make the transhistorical meaning of the historical events that underlie the Christian faith a meaning whose true reference is eschatological and whose compulsion is exerted in the existential situation created by Christian preaching. I have felt compelled to ask whether this is adequate. It has seemed to me that the historical events themselves on which the Christian faith is grounded, and therefore also a knowledge of those events in their actual happening, must be accorded a determining position in any statement of the Christian faith.

Thirdly, the Bishop points to Dietrich Bonhoeffer as the one who more than anyone else wrestled with the

---

helps to put side by side with this the comment made by John Lawrence in his review of *Honest to God* where he says: "It seems to be assumed throughout that what 'modern man' can or cannot believe is the test of truth. . . . Christianity is not easy for the natural man to accept in any age. Nor is mid-twentieth-century man of necessity the type of the future. In the next century man may be astonished at the confidence of our current disbeliefs." (*Frontier,* Summer, 1963.)

[4] "My faith," says Julian Huxley, "is in the possibilities of man." (*Christianity and Naturalism,* p. 239.)

questions raised by religionless man. But here I have felt compelled to ask whether the Bishop is truly interpreting Bonhoeffer. The misunderstanding becomes clear when the Bishop identifies Bonhoeffer's teaching of "the Beyond in our midst" with Tillich's concept of self-transcendence and, what is more misleading, thinks that because D. H. Lawrence uses language similar to that of Bonhoeffer, Lawrence can serve as a bridge by which religionless man can be led to an understanding of Bonhoeffer's message to him (*Honest to God,* pp. 120–121. Hereafter abbreviated HG). It has seemed to me that, whereas Bonhoeffer's essential protest is against religion as such, against the attitude of "God for man," Bishop Robinson construes it as a protest that supports that denial of God which man "come of age" makes because he feels he does not need God anymore. Therefore, the Bishop desires to show why man still needs God and in what sense he does, whereas Bonhoeffer is seeking to help man see God's need of him.

Even though I have ventured in these ways to be critical of some of the basic positions taken by the Bishop, I want to say that he is eminently right in selecting these very problems for discussion. As he points out, there is no real answer to the present malaise among many intellectuals in the West, and no real help for them in their loss of faith in the Christian verities, in any recall to religion or in any attempts at religious revival as commonly understood. The problem and the need are too deep for that.

There are two things the Bishop thinks should be done. First, the church should "equip Christians, by the quality and power of its community life, to enter with their 'secret discipline' into all the exhilarating and dangerous, secular strivings of our day, there to follow and to find the workings of God" (HG, p. 139). Secondly, we need to face the issue that "this basic commitment to Christ

may have been in the past—and may be for most of us
still—buttressed and fortified by many lesser commit-
ments—to a particular projection of God, a particular
'myth' of the Incarnation, a particular code of morals, a
particular pattern of religion. Without the buttresses it
may look as if all would collapse. Nevertheless, we must
beware of clinging to the buttresses instead of to Christ,
and still more must we beware of insisting on the buttresses as the way to Christ. For to growing numbers in
our generation they are barriers rather than supports."
(HG, pp. 140–141.) With both these basic concerns
most will agree.

Indeed, it is because of that agreement that I have attempted to do in this sequel to the Bishop's book what the
Bishop himself has done in his own book: and that is to
rely so heavily on the writings of others. "In this book,
more than in any other I have written," says the Bishop,
"I am struggling to think other people's thoughts after
them" (HG, p. 21). I have done the same, except that
the thinkers who are represented in this sequel are those
whom I find convincing and who have a right to be heard
in this discussion because they too have wrestled precisely with the same problems. To the memory of one
of them—John Baillie—this book is affectionately dedicated. He influenced my life and thought in many ways.
One of my proud possessions is an autographed copy of
his book *A Diary of Private Prayer*,[5] in which he wrote:
"There is nobody to whom I have felt myself closer in
Christian fellowship and theological reflection during the
last several years than my dear friend D. T. Niles."

Let me mention, here, some of those whom I have
quoted extensively in this book, and why: John Baillie,
who helps the Christian to see that he does not have to
buy the ways of thinking of the scientist, the humanist,
and the logical positivist on their own terms; Karl Barth,
who, apart from his polemics against natural theology,

[5] Charles Scribner's Sons, 1949.

demonstrates the impossibility of including Jesus Christ in any theological understanding except as such understanding is grounded in Him alone and arises out of an acceptance of Him only as Lord; Donald Baillie, whose exposition of the incarnation and atonement shows how these events are truly congruent with the nature of human existence; Hendrik Kraemer, whose rigorous maintenance of the distance between theism in all its forms and faith in God as it is in Jesus Christ helps to clear away all sentimentalism and half-truths in one's understanding of the religions; Visser 't Hooft, who demonstrates the life-and-death nature of the church's struggle with all forms of syncretism; and Reinhold Niebuhr, whose treatment of the Christian ethic is more profound than that of any other because he maintains without wearying the tense dialectic between law and grace, justice and love.

It is impossible to forget that there is another book by Bishop Robinson, entitled *In the End, God,* which in many ways throws light on his present book. In the first book he maintains the universalist position; in *Honest to God* he shows that universalism is the only conclusion that is consistent with theism. It is difficult to refute the Bishop's argument as an argument, but it is necessary to say that in his conclusion he goes beyond the Biblical teaching. It is impossible on the basis of the New Testament to say, "I know that at the end all men will be saved," just as it is impossible on the New Testament evidence to say, "I know at the end some men will be damned." This situation, in which the New Testament leaves us, is the only situation within which it is possible to proclaim, on the one hand, that God's love for men in Christ is the inescapable and unfailing ground of their being and, on the other hand, that each man's destiny is bound up with his answer to God in Jesus Christ.

To put it crudely, the difficulties that Bishop Robinson creates for those who already believe in Jesus Christ are the result of using his life, death, resurrection, and ascension as yielding categories for a religious understanding of human existence rather than as constituting God's meeting ground with man. This is why the Bishop, in both the books we have mentioned, does not raise the questions: Must men believe in Jesus Christ as Lord? and, Must they be baptized into the body of believers and bear his name? When the necessity of an answer to Jesus, in the terms set out by the New Testament, is blurred, does it then make a difference whether one talks of religionless man or religious man? The Christian man has to be religionless man because he has to demonstrate the fact that to say "Yes" to Jesus means a full involvement with Jesus in the secular world. A Christian has also to be religious man, because he will need through the practices of religion to renew his commitment to Jesus Christ and to fortify that commitment by those religious practices which are provided for him within the life of the Christian community. That so many religious men are not, at the same time, religionless men is what worried Bonhoeffer. That so many religionless men are so religious but without a knowledge of how to freshen the springs of their obedience is equally worrying. But neither of these worries has any significance if there is no distinction between Christian man and the man who is not a Christian.

The demonstration of the truth and contemporary significance of the Christian gospel and its demand lies in the Christian community. The Christian community is intended to press the question, What have you done about what God has done for you in Jesus Christ? It is also intended to show by its life what it means to answer this question, and to teach men how to maintain within life those practices by which the experience of being questioned and the experience of giving the answer can be kept alive, renewed, and refreshed. The point that needs to be made, again and again, is that it is not enough to speak of the obligation to love and of meeting the obligations of love as if we know what this means. It is essential in one's life to hold this command to love in conjunction with the command to believe in Jesus Christ.

How is it that we can talk of faith in Jesus Christ? It is because a group of men and women who encountered the Christ event were captured by it and declared that in it was the paradigm by which all of life was to be explained. It is also because these men enshrined this faith in a life lived in common. "Religion," says Karl Barth, "is perhaps a private matter. But we are speaking here not of religion but of faith, and that cannot be a private matter."[6] Faith is the faith of a community; the individual's faith is the way in which he exercises his membership in that community. Had Bishop Robinson given to the community nature of the origin, content, and quality of the Christian faith its determinative significance, we would have had a book in which there was a sharper insistence on the cruciality of the life of Jesus as it was actually lived, a fuller consideration of worship and prayer as belonging to a life lived in common, and a more radical understanding of the total history of the human community as itself pointing to the Lordship of Jesus Christ.

Bishop Robinson makes a point of the fact that in the Gospels, "Jesus never claims to be God, personally: yet he always claims to bring God, completely" (HG, p. 73). This is true as pointing to one side of the mystery of the incarnation—the Word become flesh—for the incarnation does not mean that we can say, "Jesus of Nazareth is identical with God." But there is also the other side of the mystery to which the incarnation points, that Jesus rightly claims not simply to bring God, but to be God to

[6] Karl Barth, *The Knowledge of God and the Service of God* (Alec R. Allenson, Inc., 1955; Hodder & Stoughton, Ltd., London, 1938), p. 154.

man—to say what God alone has the right to say to him,
to do what God alone can do for him. He forgave sins; he
claimed to be the bearer of the new age; he demonstrated
his power over nature and over death; he issued the
command, "Follow me"; he said that on men's attitude to
him their final destiny depended. Bishop Robinson suggests that men saw through Him into God (here was a
window into God at work) (HG, p. 71), the New
Testament witness is that "men saw him."

In the Gospel story, when John the Baptist sent his
disciples to Jesus with the question, "Are you he who is
to come?", the answer that Jesus gave them was: "Go and
tell John what you see and hear: the blind receive their
sight and the lame walk, lepers are cleansed and the deaf
hear, and the dead are raised up, and the poor have good
news preached to them" (Matt. 11:3–5). If these things
did not actually happen, there was no point in the answer;
but if they did happen, then the import of the announcement that the Kingdom had arrived was that a larger and
more abundant life had crashed into this world and lifted
its possibilities. It is meaningless to deny "the divine
event" and to claim that all events are "natural" and that
their transcendent quality simply resides in a transcendent purpose. The latter is true without making the
former untrue. It is not even of Christ himself, but of
those called by him to discipleship, that A. G. Hogg has
made this comment: "If I am really and exclusively on
the business of the Divine King, all the resources of our
Father's empire of Reality must needs be at my call for
the legitimate requirements of my errand. That he who
is on the King's business should have the right to work
miracles at need is no subject for surprise or incredulity.
The real marvel is elsewhere; it lies in the fact that we
mortals should actually be entrusted with the King's
business."[7]

[7] A. G. Hogg, *Christian Message to the Hindu* (SCM Press,
Ltd., London, 1947), p. 65.

It may be that, as an Asian living in a part of the world in which the experience of human existence and its possibilities being transcended is a part of common life, I have not felt the pressure of the task that Bishop Robinson has set himself. "The task," he says, "is to validate the idea of transcendence for modern man." (HG, p. 44.) But however experienced in East or West, it is true that the transcendent has to be made meaningful in speech as well. "The language of 'transcendence,' " Bishop Robinson quotes R. W. Hepburn as saying, "the thought of God as a personal being, wholly other to man, dwelling in majesty—this talk may well collapse into meaninglessness, in the last analysis." (HG, p. 40.) G. F. Woods, who begins his instructive essay on "The Idea of the Transcendent" with those words of Hepburn, concludes: "I do not know whether the phrase 'last analysis' means the last analysis which is made before human inquiry for some reason comes to an end or whether it means that we may reach an analysis which shows with finality that the language of transcendence has collapsed or must collapse. I do not myself think that such an analysis has yet been made and I think it is unlikely that it will be or can be made."[8] The search for language must go on, the experience itself is self-validating.

I have one concern as I send this manuscript for publication. I have written it under the conviction that the discussion of the issues that Bishop Robinson has thrust into the foreground of public debate cannot be allowed to rest where the Bishop has left them. I have also written it in the hope that at least some of the very many who have read the Bishop's book will find in these pages a probing of the Christian faith that helps to make clear to them what the challenges of that faith are. I have no desire to defend outmoded or unhelpful categories of thought or modes of expression: but no one committed to proclaim a message that calls men to repentance and

[8] In A. R. Vidler, ed., *Soundings*, p. 65.

faith can do less than seek to make the message plain with that intent.

I have called this book "We Know in Part." (I Cor. 13:9.) This is not simply a humble recognition of the status of human knowledge. It is also a confession of faith. Dostoevsky once said: "It is not like a child that I believe in Christ and confess Him. My hosanna has come forth from the crucible of doubt." God the Father of our Lord Jesus Christ is a mystery whom we confess when we say "We know" and that "We know in part." We may not be as those "who bring their god in their hand" (Job 12:6).

1

"We Know in Part"

JOHN McINTYRE begins his book *On the Love of God* with the following paragraph:

> Every book has its generating situation. It may be some experience which throws light on a scene of previous difficulty, and opens up the way ahead to new solutions. Or the reverse may happen. The experience may create problems where the issues previously seemed clear. Either way, to know the generating situation is already to have begun to share the perspective of the writer, and to be testing the authenticity of his premises, and his conclusions.[1]

It has been a practice of my life, for the last many years, to choose a book of the Bible to live with for a fairly long time. The book I have lived with for the last eighteen months has been The Psalms. It has been a solemn and solemnizing experience to enter with the psalmists into the many human moods in which they approached God and spoke to him. But the question was always present why the dominant situation out of which most of the psalmists sang their songs was one of inquiry. There was little questioning about the reliability of God.

[1] John McIntyre, *On the Love of God* (Harper & Row, Publishers, Inc., 1962; William Collins Sons & Co., Ltd., London, 1962).

He was faithful and trustworthy beyond all cavil. To
think of him and of all that he had already done was to
praise him and hold on to him. And yet, how often this
praise and trust were a "nevertheless."

> Nevertheless I am continually with thee;
>   thou dost hold my right hand. . . .
> My flesh and my heart may fail,
>   but God is the strength of my heart
>   and my portion for ever.
>
> (Ps. 73:23,26.)
>
> Why are you cast down, O my soul,
>   and why are you disquieted within me?
> Hope in God; for I shall again praise him,
>   my help and my God.
>
> (Ps. 42:5.)

Faith was secure because God was known. He was the
God of their fathers. He was the God who wrought their
deliverance from bondage. He was the God who made
heaven and earth. And yet this faith had constantly to
contend with the experiences of dereliction and of repro-
bation.

> How long, O Lord? Wilt thou hide thyself for ever?
> How long will thy wrath burn like fire?
>
> (Ps. 89:46.)
>
> Thou didst hide thy face,
>   I was dismayed. . . .
> "Hear, O Lord, and be gracious to me!
> O Lord, be thou my helper!"
>
> (Ps. 30:7,10.)

It was impossible to live with this constant note of
inquiry in The Psalms without at the same time being
nourished by its expressions of faith. But the point always
was that the inquiring spirit had not itself found that
faith. That faith was secure only because it was an experience not so much of holding as of being held, not so
much of finding as of being found.

For thou, O Lord, art my hope,
    my trust, O Lord, from my youth.
Upon thee I have leaned from my birth;
    thou art he who took me from my mother's womb. . . .
I have been as a portent to many.

(Ps. 71:5–7.)

I was in the midst of this study of The Psalms when I read the book *Honest to God,* by Bishop Robinson. I shall have a great deal to say about his book later, but the observation I want to make now is that on its first reading it seemed to say to me the exact opposite of what the psalmists had said. It seemed to say: "You must forget all this business about God acting. God is Being, and the only thing you know about this beingness of God is that he is the ground of your being. You will have many experiences in relation to that ground, the chief of which will be that you and the ground of your being are inseparable. The wholeness of your life lies in the discovery that this inseparable relation is also a relation of acceptance: an acceptance that is experienced and expressed in the normal relationships of daily life in the world."

The purpose of this book I am writing is to make clear to myself and to others the real thrust of what Bishop Robinson is trying to say, and to learn from him. It is also to contend with him for a statement of the Christian faith in more adequate categories than he chooses. But let it be the purpose of this first chapter to ask, in the terms in which the psalmists speak, what the relation should be between one's faith grounded in the faithfulness of God and one's knowledge of him which is so obviously partial. "In the wisdom of God the world by wisdom knew not God." (I Cor. 1:21.) Indeed, it is the fragmentary nature of man's knowledge of God that defines the situation for all who desire to speak honestly of him.

In his book, Bishop Robinson quotes from an article by Bishop Pike, of California, in which the Bishop says:

> I stand in a religious tradition . . . which really does not know very much about religion. The Roman Catholics and the Southern Baptists know a great deal more about religion than we do. And . . . I feel that many people within my own church—and some of them write tracts for the book-stalls of churches—know too many answers. I do not deny the truth of these answers; I simply don't know as much as the authors of the pamphlets. (HG, p. 20.)

Reading this, I was reminded of a saying in one of the Bindle books in which Joseph Bindle, a good-hearted Cockney who did not believe in "Church," complained to one of his friends about his Puritan wife, that she had more knowledge of God than she had a right to. "It is not decent," was his comment.

> I have heard students [says Prof. Eugen Rosenstock-Huessy] talking about the attributes of God in a way that made me feel ashamed. They knew everything "about" God, except that He was listening to them.[2]

No, it is not very much that we can say about God directly. But the point is that what we can say and what we cannot say are both held within his own acts of disclosure. Archbishop Ramsey, in his little book *Image Old and New,* in which he meets some of the difficulties raised by Bishop Robinson, quotes himself as saying in his mission at Oxford in 1960:

> I am going to be speaking about God. You would expect that. But I am not at the outset going to use the word "God." This is because the word has become conventional, and I am asking you to think about a reality

[2] Quoted by J. H. Oldham in his book *Life Is Commitment* (Harper & Row, Publishers, Inc., 1953; SCM Press, Ltd., London, 1953), p. 47.

rather than a word. It is also because I want to suggest that I am talking about what is already going on inside you, and not about a sort of outside technicality which I have come to sell to you.[3]

When one reads the accounts of modern atheism, . . . [says John Oldham] one cannot escape the feeling that what modern atheism is revolting against is, in part at least, the objectified God, conceived by the atheists, as by many Christians, as an immensely magnified human person, with whom men can talk on equal terms and arraign His government of the world. But that . . . is not God, but an idol and, in so far as modern atheism destroys that idol, it is doing a service to true religion.[4]

When we are talking about God, we are talking about, to use Archbishop Ramsey's words, "what is already going on inside us." God is busy with us all. Some recognize and accept God's hold on them and identify him by a whole story, the story of all that he has done.

The Story of the word "God" is that it has no given meaning but acquires a meaning in history, as it is presented in the Bible in many ways. There are always people who are saying: "It is He again; it is the Name." And then history is made, humanity progresses, and the perspective of hope is revealed. So it is better not to pronounce the Name of God, especially that sacred Name of four letters in the Old Testament which Orthodox Jews never say. The Name is not a doctrine: it is a power overwhelming human reality, but within history, not as a metaphysical control. It is "God with us" [Immanu-El]. "God with us" is a Name which manifests itself not in a supernatural but in a normal way, as a new meaning of daily events. The

[3] Michael Ramsey, *Image Old and New* (S.P.C.K., London, 1963). Reprinted by Forward Movement Publications with the permission of S.P.C.K.

[4] Oldham, *op. cit.,* p. 47.

visit to Abraham by the Lord and two angels seems
to us like a supernatural event, but it is in fact a
quite natural story within the area of myth. In the
primitive world of that time a stranger was a godhead.
So it was quite natural that the three divine powers
should come as strangers. But what was not natural,
and what made history, was that Abraham said, "It is
the Name again; it is He who spoke with me."[5]

This is what is meant when we speak of "revelation"
and of "grace." It is the insistence that, since God is love
and is personal, the initiative does not come from us but
from thence. To use the words of Karl Barth: "He makes
Himself known through Himself by distinguishing Himself *in* the world *from* the world."[6]

Hence arises the certitude of faith providing the context within which the many questions of doubt are raised.
As John Baillie has put it, "the concept of faith always
contains both the idea of knowing and the idea of not
knowing fully."[7]

"We shall know fully," says Paul. "For now we see in
a mirror dimly, but then face to face. Now I know in
part; then I shall understand fully, even as I have been
fully understood." (I Cor. 13:12.) That "I have been
fully understood" is my standing ground. All my efforts
to understand arise out of the fact that I am understood
rather than out of my own understanding. That is why
in the Christian life our knowledge of God, such as we
have or such as we think we have, cannot take the place
of God himself, the object of that knowledge. Says John
Baillie:

> It is God himself, as he comes to meet us in Christ, of
> whom the Christian is indefeasibly certain, and not

[5] Article by Professor van Peursen in *Student World*, No. 1,
1963, p. 21.
[6] Barth, *The Knowledge of God and the Service of God*, p. 21.
[7] John Baillie, *The Sense of the Presence of God*, p. 5.

such statements as he can make about God; and the degree of his assurance in holding to such statements will vary directly with the degree of their proximity to, or remoteness from, the elements of reflective insight already present, in however latent a form, in faith's own awareness of the God who thus comes to meet him.[8]

This whole position is very important, because increasing knowledge itself is dependent on the obedience that springs from faith, and obedience has to be rendered to God. No wonder Paul, writing to the Galatians about their obedience, corrects his own argument in these words: "but now that you have come to know God, or rather to be known by God, how can you . . . " (Gal. 4:9).

The seers of Hindu India spoke of God as a mystery concerning whom men had their "darshans," their glimpses of his presence. These darshans are partial; what is determinative for the Christian is that the mystery of God is not a mystery of darkness but of light. Indeed, the mystery remains, for the light is unbearable. It is light, nevertheless. For God has laid his hold on me. "Not that I have already obtained this or am already perfect; but I press on to make it my own, because Christ Jesus has made me his own." (Phil. 3:12.)

Certainly, all questions concerning this act of God in Christ are not answered. There remains what the theologians have called "the mystery of God's sovereign liberty." But it is the mystery of a good God. As Pierre Maury has so finely said:

He [God] wills to act only in accordance with his good pleasure (Phil. 2.13), but it is a *good* pleasure. His entire revelation tells us so, tirelessly. There is nothing higher than his goodness, nor anterior to it. God *loves always,* from all eternity. And his purpose, before which, and outside which, there is none other, is to

[8] *Ibid.,* pp. 91–92.

ally his life with the life of men in mutual love. Often
moved by their adoration of the divine majesty, the
great predestinarian doctors—especially Calvin—have
exalted the mystery of the *absolute decree*. But why
have they turned it into a mystery as impenetrable as
night, the secret of an opaque God? God does not
live and act in the obscurity of eternal darkness, but
in light—"unapproachable," yes, but light![9]

If, at the very beginning of our argument, we emphasize this act of God in Christ on me, it is because it is out
of this act that faith is born and the Christian receives
the right to talk about God and what he knows about him.
The act of God in Christ on me is for me the present tense
of the God who is the same yesterday, today, and forever.
My story and what has happened to me have no meaning
apart from all that God has done for all mankind. My
experience of God in Christ, instead of imprisoning me
in solipsism, sets me within an area of discourse that
stretches back to the beginning of time and stretches forward to the fulfillment of all history. Apart from this
gift of faith, it is impossible to know that we know, or to
speak credibly of what we know, about God.

> The test of reality [says John Baillie] is the resistance it
> offers to the otherwise uninhibited course of my own
> thinking, desiring and acting. Reality is what I "come
> up against," what takes me by surprise, the other-than-
> myself which pulls me up and obliges me to reckon
> with it and adjust myself to it because it will not con-
> sent simply to adjust itself to me.[10]

This resistance we meet within the physical world, the
world of objects. But reflection tells us that this world of
objects is always known in relation to and never apart

[9] Pierre Maury, *Predestination and Other Papers* (John Knox
Press, 1960; SCM Press, Ltd., London, 1960), p. 35.
[10] John Baillie, *The Sense of the Presence of God*, p. 35.

from the world of selves. I know the physical world only as a world common to myself and to my fellows. In the words of W. E. Hocking:

> I do not first know my physical world as a world of *objects,* and then as a world of *shared* objects: it is through a prior recognition of the presence of other mind that my physical experience acquires objectivity at all. The objectivity of nature is its community.[11]

This is why the experience of "resistance" and the experience of "presence" belong together in our experience of reality: and presence is a property that properly belongs to the relation between selves. An illustration of this point is given by John Baillie in his discussion of the significance of the preposition "with": "A chair may be beside me in the room, but I should not say that a chair was with me, still less perhaps that I was with a chair. It is only persons that I can be with."[12]

But just as my knowledge of the reality of the physical world points to the world of selves, even so this world of selves points beyond itself to a greater reality. In fact, it is this very signification beyond themselves that gives to those selves their own intrinsic meaning.

> If "others are the real world," it is because they embody for me, in my encounter with them, something greater than themselves, an intrinsic right and a universal good. My relations with my fellows have the significance of reality for me only because and in so far as they mediate to this greater reality. . . . To all those who have not entirely surrendered their hold upon religious truth, this greater reality is God.[13]

[11] W. E. Hocking, *The Meaning of God in Human Experience* (Yale University Press, 1912; Oxford University Press, London, 1912), p. 288.
[12] John Baillie, *The Sense of the Presence of God,* pp. 35–36.
[13] *Ibid.,* pp. 36–37.

Arnold Toynbee speaks of three attitudes that are common to what he calls the higher religions. This is how he expresses them:

> First of all, in their attitude toward Man, the higher religions all agree, I believe, in feeling, and feeling intensely, that Man is not the spiritually highest presence known to Man. . . . Next let us consider the attitude toward evil. I think that, here again, there are two points in which all religions agree. The first point is that they all feel that Man ought to take sides with good against evil. . . . A second point is that Man must try to place himself in harmony with that Spiritual presence in the Universe that is spiritually greater than Man—a presence that, in personal terms, reveals itself as god, and, in its impersonal facet, as absolute reality. . . . Lastly, we have to consider the attitude towards the problem of suffering. The attitude towards suffering is an attitude that underlies theological beliefs. It also underlies, and perhaps eventually determines, conduct and practice.[14]

Here we have a rather neat description of the coordinates within which we may possess our knowledge of the real, and it sets forward clearly the importance of recognizing that all experience of the world of objects, of the world of selves, and of the ultimate presence belong together and determine both belief and conduct. To deny any one element is to lose the whole. What such a loss can mean is expressed strikingly by M. Satre, for whom that loss had taken place.

> The existentialist finds it very troublesome that God does not exist, because with Him disappears all possibility of finding values in an intelligible world; nor can there be any a priori good, because there is no infinite or perfect consciousness of it; nor is it anywhere

[14] Arnold Toynbee, *Christianity Among the Religions of the World* (Charles Scribner's Sons, 1957; Oxford University Press, London, 1958), pp. 20–24.

written that good exists, that we ought to be honest and not tell lies; for we are precisely on a plane where nothing exists but men. . . . I am very much vexed that this should be so, but if I have suppressed God the Father, there must be somebody to invent values.[15]

But, and this is where the argument turns upon itself, the path to the knowledge of the real through the experiences of resistance and of presence, through the facts of community and of commitment, is in the last analysis a path to no one and to nowhere, unless he who is on this path is already a person who has arrived at his destination by the miracle of grace and faith. The psalmist could not help describing himself as "a portent" (Ps. 71:7). He was inexplicable in other terms.

Hendrik Kraemer, discussing the classic Vedantist position of Sankara on the relation between the Atman and the Brahman, observes that where the determining interest is the path the Atman must take to find "release," there

"God" is, in principle, a means, and man is the centre and meaning of the whole process. . . . *Atman* swallows *Brahman*. This radical anthropocentrism bereaves "God" of all real significance, so that not only from the angle of logical thinking, but also from that of . . . "religious cleanness," atheism must be considered the most appropriate position.[16]

This conclusion in atheism is what the Buddha propounded. "He is," in the words of Kraemer, "still the Unanswered Question which arose out of the logic of India's own spiritual life."[17]

[15] M. Satre, *L'Existentialisme est un Humanisme*, pp. 35, 89 (quoted by John Baillie, *The Sense of the Presence of God*, p. 38).
[16] Hendrik Kraemer, *Religion and the Christian Faith* (The Westminster Press, 1957; Lutterworth Press, London, 1956), p. 110.
[17] *Ibid.*, p. 115.

Bishop Robinson has in his book a chapter entitled "The End of Theism?" The question mark in the title finds no answer in the chapter, for the problem with which the chapter deals is that of the conception of the transcendence of God and it is treated as a problem in "conceiving." Theism, in the Christian sense, stands or falls not with any particular way in which we can conceive of God's transcendence but in the reality of what we have called "the action of God," in which God takes the initiative and where that action includes the act of grace as well as the gift of faith. Where the initiative is with God, there is theism; where the initiative is with man, whether this be understood in existentialist or Vedantist terms, there is atheism: and by no amount of poetry in the language used can the difference be hidden.

"I believe" is man's response in commitment and obedience to God's gracious action on him and on his behalf. "I know" is man's affirmation within the terms of his experience of "the Really Real," as that reality is mediated to him in his relation to other selves within their shared world. Always when he says "I believe," he also has to add "Help thou my unbelief." Always when he says "I know," he also has to add "I know in part." And the two, faith and knowledge, go hand in hand, knowledge providing faith with the means of its obedience and faith illumining knowledge with wisdom.

2

In the Search of the Depth

DIFFERENT PEOPLE like different ways of cooking. For instance, there are many ways in which eggs can be served at table. They can be served as a main course; or eggs that have been boiled and cut into small pieces can be used to garnish another course; or eggs can become an ingredient in a sauce that is served as a relish. There is even another possibility, that eggs be cooked into a custard of which milk is an equal ingredient.

Similarly, the Christian faith can be presented in so many ways. But where it simply garnishes another course, or is only used as a relish, its own purpose and integrity are compromised. Syncretism is the attempt to serve it as a custard. The Christian faith is meant to be a main course. Indeed, it is meant to be the complete meal. Honesty always asks the question with regard to any presentation of the faith, "Has the faith itself been truly communicated and made clear?"

By his book *Honest to God*, Bishop Robinson has succeeded in making the Christian faith a subject of general conversation. He has succeeded in making new ways of thought and new ideas explosive. He has removed from many people's minds unnecessary obstacles to faith. And yet the book does make people ask, "Has he succeeded in doing what he set out to do?"

He has said, "I affirm in my book as strongly as I can the utterly personal character of God. I wholly accept the doctrine of God revealed in the New Testament and enshrined in the creeds. My sole concern is to question whether the doctrine must necessarily be expressed in certain images and categories which might have the effect for many in our generation of making it unreal."[1] The real reason for this present book is that it has seemed to me, as to many others reading the Bishop's book, that while the new categories of thought which he advocates do illumine the Christian faith, they prove themselves, in the final showing, to be inadequate to communicate the very essence of that faith. Indeed, has it not been true right through the centuries, that while different categories of thought have proved adequate to prepare men for faith in God in Christ, such men have always found that, in the last analysis, they had to wrestle with the categories that the Bible itself uses to express that faith! In the Bishop's book, I myself found those parts most illuminating where he discusses why he finds some of the Biblical categories disconcerting.

John McIntyre in his book *On the Love of God*, from which we have already quoted, has an interesting discussion on the use of words.

If [he says] we hold that the "meaning" of a word is the function that word performs in living communication, then it is possible to hold that the form which the function takes may vary according to the social, economic, political and cultural conditions obtaining at the time. The word "salvation" may function as "ransom" in a slave-society, as "satisfaction" in a feudal society, as "substitution" in a Renascence society, and "reconciliation" in a society dominated by personalist categories; but in each case it is the same function which is diversified—namely, that of conquering sin by grace. It is this identity of function which each of the different

[1] From a press report, quoted in *Ecumenical Press Service*, May 17, 1963.

words serves that provides the continuity we have been seeking and is the only effective answer to a completely relativist interpretation of the situation.[2]

It is this problem of the continuity of meaning that the Bishop has underestimated, a problem all the more acute because the word he is dealing with is the word "God"; so that in terms of the new categories he wants to use he has to ensure that they perform the essential function that in Biblical faith the word "God" performs. There is practically nothing in the Bible about "God as He is." The whole drive of the Biblical faith is to make clear to men "God as He does." Oscar Cullmann puts this point in a startling way.

> Primitive Christianity [he says] knows nothing of a timeless God. The "eternal" God is he who was in the beginning, is now, and will be in all the future. . . . Accordingly, his eternity can and must be expressed in this "naive" way, in terms of endless time.[3]

God is known as our time is filled out by God. Should this "doing" become an opaque concept because of the new way in which God is defined or described, then whatever knowledge about God is communicated or whatever relation to God is established, the Biblical faith itself has been set aside. The issue is not whether men are being helped to find God, nor whether men are being helped to a faith that issues in purposeful living. The issue simply is whether men are being helped to meet God in Christ and in that meeting are led to life commitment.

The problem that the Bishop sets himself is to help those men and women who find it impossible to believe in God because for them God either means one who is

[2] McIntyre, *op. cit.*, p. 133.
[3] Oscar Cullmann, *Christ and Time* (The Westminster Press, 1950; SCM Press, Ltd., London, 1951; revised edition, 1964), p. 63.

spatially situated or he is conceived as a being distinct from other beings. They find not only that God has gradually ceased to be necessary to explain so many things that once were inexplicable without him, but also that, even in terms of man's interior life, there was little evidence of the god-shaped-gap that H. G. Wells used to talk about.

Using the Bishop's book itself as a guide, let us summarize the position that those men adopt whom the Bishop is trying to help.

1. *They deny that God is up there.*

The cosmogony implicit in much of the Bible has been outmoded for a long time, but is it a fact that in the Bible any truth or argument is dependent on that cosmogony? Can R. Gregor Smith establish his statement that "the old doctrine of transcendence is nothing more than an assertion of an outmoded view of the world"?[4] The simple fact is that the teaching on transcendence in the Bible was not an assertion about the world at all, but an assertion about God made by men whose view of the world is now outmoded.

This need not even mean that the words they used are outmoded. For instance, the words "up" and "down" are simple spatial words, so that even though originally they had a spatial reference they were not tied to that reference. Let me give a modern example. The first railway in Ceylon was from Colombo to Kandy. Kandy is in the hills, so that the train from Colombo to Kandy was the "up-train." The train from Kandy to Colombo was the "down-train." Now, every train to Colombo is a down-train, irrespective of how up or down the train starts from. Similarly, the words "ascended" and "descended" which are used to describe the person and work of Jesus

[4] Smith, *op. cit.,* p. 108. Quoted by Bishop Robinson, HG, p. 44.

Christ are quite independent of a three-decker conception of the universe: as independent as when at Oxford they talk about a student being "sent down."

Words have derivations and histories, but in daily usage they carry their own meaning. In fact, should any-one say that he cannot accept the Christian faith because some of the terminology is derived from a three-decker conception of the universe, one must be forgiven if he strongly suspects that the reason given for unfaith is only an excuse. It is certainly all to the good if this excuse can be removed, but too much attention paid to the excuse is unhelpful.

The real difficulty lies in the fact that the primary mode of Biblical expression is much nearer to drama than to any systematic exposition in categories of reflective thought, so that those who insist that God must be off-stage find the naïveté of the Bible disconcerting. "God up there" is not an affirmation that that is where God is; it is an affirmation that he comes and that he can be seen at work on the stage of life. There are those who would decry this anthropomorphism of the Bible, but they forget that the anthropomorphic way of speaking is the way of man's direct speech. The circumlocutions of philosophy have their own reason and their own validity, but the language of the Bible is not pre-philosophical in the philosophical sense but in the human sense.

Kraemer in his discussion of Paul Tillich speaks of "his not precisely formulated but adumbrated tendency to take Biblical religion as a pre-philosophical stage of thinking." Kraemer remarks:

> Up to a certain point, one can say that Biblical think-ing is one of the forms of pre-philosophical thinking, if one puts it simply under the heading of "classifica-tion of types of thinking," on the assumption that the philosophical is the normative pattern of thinking. However, if one takes Biblical thinking according to its

peculiar nature and spirit, it is entirely a type of its own, and wholly unphilosophical, even often anti-philosophical. In this light the whole justification for considering Biblical thinking a pre-philosophical stage of thinking is baseless and misleading.[5]

And, in another place, discussing certain points in C. H. Dodd's commentary on the letter to the Romans, Kraemer says:

He fights shy of anthropomorphism, evidently assuming that anthropomorphic ways of speaking are (although unavoidable to a certain extent) by definition of inferior rank in comparison with more spiritualized forms: an assumption which, it seems to me, especially in the field of religious epistemology, is generally speaking a misconception. At any rate, if anthropomorphic language is somehow a blemish or inferior in status, then the Bible sits from beginning to end on the bench of the defendants.[6]

2. *They deny that God is out there.*

Bishop Robinson explains what is meant by the mental picture of a "God out there" in the following words:

Every one of us lives with some mental picture of a God "out there," a God who "exists" above and beyond the world he made, a God "to" whom we pray and to whom we "go" when we die. In traditional Christian theology, the doctrine of the Trinity witnesses to the self-subsistence of this divine Being outside us and apart from us. The doctrine of creation asserts that at a moment of time this God called "the world" into existence over against himself. The Biblical record describes how he proceeds to enter into contact with those whom he has made, how he establishes a "covenant" with them, how he "sends" to them his prophets, and

[5] Kraemer, *op. cit.*, p. 429.
[6] *Ibid.*, pp. 291–292.

how in the fullness of time he "visits" them in the person of his Son, who must one day "come again" to gather the faithful to himself. (HG, p. 14.)

The alternative to this way of thinking which is suggested is set out in a quotation from Tillich.

The name of this infinite and inexhaustible depth and ground of all being is *God*. That depth is what the word *God* means. And if that word has not much meaning for you, translate it, and speak of the depths of your life, of the source of your being, of your ultimate concern, of what you take seriously without any reservation. Perhaps, in order to do so, you must forget everything traditional that you have learned about God, perhaps even that word itself. For if you know that God means depth, you know much about him. You cannot then call yourself an atheist or unbeliever. For you cannot think or say: Life has no depth! Life is shallow. Being itself is surface only. If you could say this in complete seriousness, you would be an atheist; but otherwise you are not. He who knows about depth knows about God.[7]

Tillich is quoted again as making the same point in relation not only to the depths of our personal life but to the deepest springs of our social and historical existence.

The name of this infinite and inexhaustible ground of history is *God*. That is what the word means, and it is that to which the words *Kingdom of God* and *Divine Providence* point. And if these words do not have much meaning for you, translate them, and speak of the depth of history, of the ground and aim of our social life, and of what you take seriously without reservation in your

[7] Paul Tillich, *The Shaking of the Foundations* (Pelican Publishing Company, 1962), pp. 63 f. Originally published by Charles Scribner's Sons, 1945. Reprinted with the permission of Charles Scribner's Sons.

moral and political activities. Perhaps you should call
this depth *hope*, simply hope. For if you find hope in
the ground of history, you are united with the great
prophets who were able to look into the depth of their
times, who tried to escape it, because they could not
stand the horror of their visions, and who yet had the
strength to look to an even deeper level and there to
discover hope.[8]

All this is well said and movingly said, and yet one
wonders what the real implication is of this way of saying
it. As Bishop Robinson explains it, one must cease to talk
about God as "the highest Being" as "a person." As Tillich
puts it, we may not say that God exists. One must talk
instead of one's own experience of depth, of one's own
experience of hope. God is ultimate reality, so that it is
not possible to speak of ultimate reality as existing, it is
only possible to discern it in one's own existence. It is in
this transition to man's central role as searching for and
experiencing his relation to the ground of his being, and
of knowing that this ground is also the ground of all being
and of all history, that there lies the distinguishing mark
of what the Bishop is talking about.

There is a real problem here, for while the divine
presence is indeed mediated through human experience,
an essential part of that experience is the recognition that
it is God himself who does it. It is this recognition that
finds expression in the words "God exists." Apart from
this, "God" is no more a noun but an adjective, a quality
of human existence. It is against this consequence that
Barth issues his warning lest "we would have defined in
one way or another the essence of that which is not God,
we would have defined the creature, and in the end the
essence of man himself."[9]

The Bible's insistence on the "God out there" is in
order to point to God as the one who, in the last analysis,

[8] *Ibid.*, pp. 65 f.
[9] Barth, *The Knowledge of God and the Service of God*, p. 33.

apprehends man. The last issue is never what I take seriously without reservation or that which is my ultimate concern. The issue always is that I find myself being taken seriously and set in the midst of a history in which God's ultimate concerns constitute the very texture of life.

There is real poignancy in the cry, which Bishop Robinson echoes, for a God who is not "above it all," for a God who is concerned and is involved. But were there not also at the same time a relation between man and God above him, man would lose his childhood. The problem for most men is not that they have become orphans, but that they have become adults.

3. *They deny the God who is the God for me.*

The significance of this denial is well set out in the following quotation from Dietrich Bonhoeffer which the Bishop gives:

> The God who makes us live in this world without using him as a working hypothesis is the God before whom we are ever standing. Before God and with him we live without God. God allows himself to be edged out of the world, and that is exactly the way, the only way, in which he can be with us and help us. . . . This is the decisive difference between Christianity and all religions. Man's religiosity makes him look in his distress to the power of God in the world; he uses God as a *Deus ex machina*. The Bible however directs him to the powerlessness and suffering of God; only a suffering God can help. To this extent we may say that the process we have described by which the world came of age was an abandonment of a false conception of God, and a clearing of the decks for the God of the Bible, who conquers power and space in the world by his weakness. This must be the starting point for our "worldly" interpretation.[10]

[10] Bonhoeffer, *Letters and Papers from Prison*, p. 164.

In this quotation from Bonhoeffer we hear the authentic voice of Biblical faith, the faith by which Christian heroes have lived at all times. But by his use of this quotation, Bishop Robinson does two things. First, he papers over the crack that his use of the Tillichian categories has caused, and secondly, he proposes to dismiss, with the aid of Bonhoeffer's protest against God as *Deus ex machina,* the God of the Bible to whom men turn in their distress.

What the Tillichian categories have done is to make God an adjective with which to describe certain types of human experience. What Bonhoeffer does is to deny that God can be used thus adjectivally. God, according to the Bible, is a suffering God, and into this life of God in the world man must enter. The attempt of religious man is to inveigle God to enter his religious life and it is this attempt which must be given up. What Bishop Robinson does is to seek to persuade us that Tillich and Bonhoeffer are talking about the same thing.

When Bonhoeffer protests against men using God as a *deus ex machina,* must that protest include men turning to God in their distress? The emphasis is right that God suffers in and for the world and that men find radical help in participating in that suffering: but it is precisely because God suffers for his world that God gives himself also to religious men in the meeting of their religious and human needs. The fact to remember is that should God be imprisoned within the religious life, the redemptive quality of his suffering is not truly experienced in the release it brings.

Let Bonhoeffer himself answer the question that he raises.

> But when all's said and done, it is true that it needs trouble to drive us to prayer, though every time I feel it is something to be ashamed of. Perhaps that is because up to now I have not had a chance of putting in a Christian word at such a moment. As we were all

lying on the floor yesterday, someone muttered "O God, O God"—he is normally a frivolous sort of chap—but I couldn't bring myself to offer him any Christian encouragement or comfort. All I did was to glance at my watch and say: "It won't last any more than ten minutes now." There was nothing premeditated about it; it came quite automatically, though perhaps I had a feeling that it was wrong to force religion down his throat just then. Incidentally, Jesus himself did not try to convert the two thieves on the cross; he waited until one of them turned to him.[11]

When one is in distress and turns to God, what does one say? There is a prayer by Bonhoeffer entitled "Prayer in Time of Distress." It is sufficient refutation of the denial of God being the God for me.

O Lord God, great is the misery that has come upon me; my cares would overwhelm me, I know not what to do. O God, be gracious unto me and help me. Grant me strength to bear what thou dost send, and let not fear rule over me. As a loving Father, take care of my loved ones my wife and children.

O merciful God, forgive me all the sins I have committed against thee, and against my fellowmen. I trust in thy grace, and commit my life wholly into thy hands, do with me as seemeth best to thee, and as is best for me. Whether I live or die, I am with thee, and thou art with me, my God. Lord, I wait for thy salvation, and for thy Kingdom. Amen.[12]

4. *They deny the God who is not me.*

It may immediately be protested that, by the employment of the new categories of thought that Bishop Robinson advocates, there is no intention whatever to identify man and God. That may be, but as Kraemer remarks:

[11] *Ibid.*, pp. 96–97.
[12] *Ibid.*, p. 70.

If God is called "Ground of Being" does there remain
a real possibility of clear distinction between Being and
its Ground, which is more than verbal declaration, and
which really allows a relation? Is not ontological philosophy always driven towards deification of Being, of the
Tò ὄv, and is it really possible to distinguish the
"Ground" clearly and meaningfully from Being? . . .
It is wholly unbiblical to speak of the "Ground of
Being," indicating by that the God of the Bible.[13]

Kraemer quotes Gunning, a Dutch theologian of the
nineteenth century, who in his exposition of Spinoza
makes the comment:

We cannot say with Spinoza: God is the Ground of the
World (Being). We must say: *in* God is the Ground
of the World. Because the world is created, is produced, it has a non-divine ground, which just for this
reason *can* become ungodly. If this were not so, then
evil would not be sin, evil, but non-being.[14]

Let us listen to what the two quotations that Bishop
Robinson gives to make his point actually say:

To call God transcendent in this sense does not mean
that one must establish a "superworld" of divine objects. It does mean that, within itself, the finite world
points beyond itself. In other words, it is self-tran-
scendent.[15]

Prayer and mystical vision are real and important, but
they cannot be the primary basis for religious conviction; this must come from *common* experience, and
special experiences like prayer are only meaningful, in
my view, insofar as they refer back to common experience. But it is one thing to say that religious propositions

[13] Kraemer, *op. cit.,* pp. 435–436.
[14] *Ibid.,* p. 436.
[15] Paul Tillich, *Systematic Theology,* Vol. II (The University
of Chicago Press, 1957; James Nisbet & Co., Ltd., London,
1957), p. 8.

can be referred to the common experience of the creative character of personal relationships: it would be
quite another to say that people commonly *recognize*
their experience of personal relationship for what it is
—an encounter with the Transcendent.[16]

In both these statements the point is truly made that
the transcendence of God is known by men within their
own experience as self-transcendence, but this self-
transcendent quality in human life and experience loses
its Biblical reference when it is forgotten that the Biblical
testimony to it is that it is the result of the graciousness of
the transcendent God. That, in my experience of others
and in my experience of myself, I find myself in touch
with a reality that I can call God is due to his grace—
the grace of Him who *chose* to be Immanuel—God with
us. To refuse the faith that the graciousness of God is
what self-transcendence points to is to refuse the Biblical
faith.

It is certainly not necessary to believe in the kind of
"superworld" that so many find untenable, nor to make
God resident there; but it is necessary to maintain that
distinction between God and man which makes it possible
to speak substantively of God. To put it in another way,
self-transcendence is dependent on transcendence itself.

5. *They deny the God who is not mine.*

Theological statements are not a description of "the
highest Being" but an analysis of the depths of personal
relationships—or, rather, an analysis of the depths of
all experience "interpreted by love." Theology, as Tillich insists, is about "that which concerns us ultimately."
A statement is "theological" not because it relates to a
particular Being called "God," but because it asks
ultimate questions about meaning of existence: it asks

[16] John Wren-Lewis, *They Became Anglicans* (A. R. Mow-
bray & Co., Ltd., London, 1950), pp. 175 f.

what, at the level of *theos,* at the level of its deepest mystery, is the reality and significance of our life. (HG, p. 49.)

Also quoting Feuerbach, Bishop Robinson writes, "This is, of course, very near to the position we have been taking."

The true atheist is not the man who denies God, the subject; it is the man for whom the attributes of divinity, such as love, wisdom and justice, are nothing. And denial of the subject is by no means necessarily denial of the attributes. (HG, p. 50.)

What is being said here is that when we talk about God we are actually talking about the nature of certain of our experiences. There is in the use of ontological categories not only the blurring of the distinction between me and God, but there is also the claim that what is mine, as a result of my reflection on my life, is what, in the last analysis, can be called "God." When challenged by Barth, that he was substituting anthropology for theology, Rudolf Bultmann answered:

I would heartily agree: I *am* trying to substitute anthropology for theology, for I am interpreting theological affirmations as assertions about human life.[17]

Only such statements about God are legitimate as express the existential relation between God and man. Statements which speak of God's actions as cosmic events are illegitimate.[18]

Bishop Robinson is no less thoroughgoing.

The necessity for the name "God" [he says] lies in the fact that our being has depths which naturalism,

[17] In *Kerygma and Myth: A Theological Debate,* ed. by H. W. Bartsch, tr. by R. H. Fuller, Vol. I (S.P.C.K., London, 1953), p. 107.
[18] Rudolf Bultmann, *Jesus Christ and Mythology* (Charles Scribner's Sons, 1958; SCM Press, Ltd., London, 1960), p. 69.

whether evolutionary, mechanistic, dialectical or hu-
manistic, cannot or will not recognize. . . . The question of God is the question *whether this depth of being
is a reality or an illusion,* not whether *a* Being exists
beyond the bright blue sky, or anywhere else. Belief in
God is a matter of "what you take seriously without any
reservation," of what for you is *ultimate* reality.

The man who acknowledges the transcendence of God
is the man who *in* the conditioned relationships of life
recognizes the unconditional and responds to it in unconditional personal relationship. (HG, pp. 54–55.)

In order that we may see the real import of what is
being claimed here, let me put alongside this conviction of
Bishop Robinson the position that Sir Radhakrishnan sets
out as the very heart of Hinduism.

Religion is not so much a revelation to be attained by
us in faith as an effort to unveil the deepest layers of
man's being and get into enduring contact with them.
Religion is more a transforming experience than a notion
of God. Religion is a natural development of a really
human life. Man, no doubt, is the measure of all things;
only his nature contains or reflects every level of reality
from matter to God.[19]

It [Hinduism] recognises the diversity in man's approach
towards, and realisation of, the one Supreme Reality.
For it the essence of religion consists in man's hold on
what is eternal and immanent in all being. Its validity
does not depend on historical happenings. The different dogmas give imaginative presentations of the basic
truth of the divine in us.[20]

The heading that we have given to this chapter is "In
the Search of the Depth." It is a phrase from the book of

[19] Sarvepalli Radhakrishnan, *Eastern Religions and Western
Thought,* 2d ed. (Oxford University Press, 1940), pp. 21, 25.
[20] Sarvepalli Radhakrishnan, *Religion and Society* (Barnes &
Noble, Inc., 2d ed., 1959; George Allen & Unwin, London,
1956), p. 52.

Job. "Hast thou walked in the search of the depth?"
(Job 38:16.) The immediate reference of the verse is to
"the recesses of the deep," but its challenge is to Job's
unconscious assumption that he knew what he was talking about when he talked about God. It is the permanent
challenge of the Bible to man's claim that, because he is
grounded in God, he has access to him apart from God's
self-disclosure.

Conclusion

> The world [says Hocking] would be consistent without
> God; it would also be consistent with God: whichever
> hypothesis a man adopts will fit experience equally well;
> neither one, so far as accounting for visible facts is con-
> cerned, works better than the other. . . . The religious
> objects (the predicates given by religion to reality)
> stand at a pass of intellectual equipoise: it may well
> seem that some other faculty must enter in to give deter-
> mination to reason at the point where reason halts,
> without deciding voice of its own.[21]

What must enter in? We have insisted that it is God
himself who must enter in, that he must make himself
known and that this is precisely what he does. We cannot
explain how it is that when men find the mystery of their
own existence and of human history illumined, they not
only affirm the wisdom that has been granted to them but
also acknowledge that it has come to them by faith in
God. They know that for them to acknowledge less would
be to deny the very substance of their illumination.

> The truth contained in the gospel [says Reinhold Nie-
> buhr] is not found in human wisdom. Yet it may be
> found at the point where human wisdom and human
> goodness acknowledge their limits; and creative despair
> induces faith. Once faith is induced it becomes truly

[21] Hocking, *op. cit.*, p. 143.

the wisdom which makes "sense" out of a life and history which would otherwise remain senseless.[22]

It must not be thought, however, that this peculiar quality belongs only to the cognitive experience of God. It belongs to cognition of every kind.

We cannot explain [says John Hick] how we are conscious of sensory phenomena as constituting an objective physical environment; we just find ourselves interpreting the data of our experience in this way. . . . Likewise we cannot explain how we know ourselves to be responsible beings subject to moral obligations; we just find ourselves interpreting our social experience in this way. . . . The same is true of the apprehension of God. The theistic believer cannot explain *how* he knows the divine presence to be mediated through his human experience. He just finds himself interpreting his experience in this way. He lives in the presence of God, though he is unable to prove by any dialectical process that God exists.[23]

It must now be clear why we have been contending for a way of thinking about God that allows, indeed insists, on an understanding of his transcendence primarily in terms of his grace. He arises, he arrives, he discloses himself, he indwells; but he is not me, not even me as the ground of my being. Yes, "in him we live and move and have our being" (Acts 17:28), that precisely is the sign of his grace, but we may not forget what this means. It does not mean that he is the ground of our being but that the ground of our being is in him.

Lest it be thought that we are trying to emphasize a distinction without a difference, let us recall the point at

[22] Reinhold Niebuhr, *The Nature and Destiny of Man*, Vol. II, *Human Destiny* (Charles Scribner's Sons, 1943; James Nisbet & Co., Ltd., London, 1941–1943), p. 206.

[23] John Hick, *Faith and Knowledge* (Cornell University Press, 1957; Oxford University Press, London, 1957), p. 132.

which Tillich himself arrives. In his article entitled "The Two Types of Philosophy of Religion," he distinguishes between two fundamental types: the ontological type, represented by the mystical tradition, and what he calls the cosmological type, represented by Thomas Aquinas and most subsequent religious thought. "The first," he says, "is based upon an underlying point of identity between man and God; the second, upon their distinct separate co-existence. On the first way Man discovers *himself* when he discovers God; he discovers something which is identical with himself. . . . On the second way, man meets a stranger when he meets God." Tillich takes his own position on the first way, and in describing it goes so far as to say: "The immediate awareness of the unconditioned has not the character of faith, but of self-evidence."

Here is the final implication of the position that Bishop Robinson pleads for. Self-discovery is God discovery and man can pass beyond the certitude of faith to the self-evidence of knowledge. Man, in search of the depth, finds.

How apposite the prayer of Augustine is: "Let us delight to find Thee by failing to find Thee, rather than to fail to find Thee by finding Thee."[24]

[24] Augustine, *Confessions*, 1.6.

CHAPTER

3

"When You Pray, Say . . ."

T HERE IS A FELICITOUS STORY that Gypsy Smith tells in one of his sermons to illustrate the relationship between man and God. One day he picked up his little son and put him on the dining table. He then stood about two yards from the table and called his son to come to him. The child walked gingerly to the edge of the table, looked at his father, then looked at the distance between the table and the father, and finally walked back and sat down. The father called him again. Again he repeated the same performance. The father called him a third time. This time he stood up, shut his eyes, and ran across the table and out into space, only to be held in the father's arms.

Every time I read the definition of God given by Tillich and quoted by Bishop Robinson, in which it was said that God was the ground of our being, my mind went back to this story of Gypsy Smith's. The father and his love were the ground of the being of the child. But the moment of faith went hand in hand with the overleaping of the distance between father and child. A distance had to be overcome.

It is this conception of distance between man and God which the Biblical categories seek to communicate. It is precisely because God is the ground of our being, or rather that the ground of our being is in God, that faith is a

55

possibility. It is also a necessity because there is distance between God and man. All forms of naturalism and pantheism deny this distance by denying the difference between God and man.

> "Naturalism" as a philosophy of life is clearly and consciously an attack on Christianity. For it the term "God" becomes interchangeable with the term "universe" and therefore is semantically superfluous.[1]

> The god hypothesis is no longer of any pragmatic value for the interpretation or comprehension of nature, and indeed often stands in the way of better and truer interpretation. Operationally, God is beginning to resemble not a ruler but the last fading smile of a cosmic Cheshire Cat.[2]

> Gods will doubtless survive, sometimes under the protection of vested interests, or in the shelter of lazy minds, or as puppets used by politicians, or as refuges for unhappy and ignorant souls.[3]

Bishop Robinson proceeds, in his book, from these quotations to a discussion of Bonhoeffer's protest against providing a sphere of religion for "unhappy people in their weakest moment." Bonhoeffer has his reason for decrying the solaces of religion. He is warning against making this kind of religious experience the basis of one's understanding of the Christian faith. But surely it is a shallow view of the Christian faith that understands Bonhoeffer as denying the Magnificat:

> He has put down the mighty from their thrones,
> and exalted those of low degree;
> he has filled the hungry with good things,
> and the rich he has sent empty away.

> (Luke 1:52–53.)

[1] Tillich, *Systematic Theology*, Vol. II, p. 7.

[2] Julian Huxley, *Religion Without Revelation* (Harper & Row, Publishers, Inc., 1957; Max Parrish & Company, Limited, London, 1957), p. 58.

[3] *Ibid.*, p. 62.

> O magnify the Lord with me,
>   With me exalt His Name;
> When in distress to Him I called,
>   He to my rescue came.
>   (From Psalm XXXIV.
>   Tate and Brady's "New Version,"
>   1696, 1698.)

Not only does Bishop Robinson take no account of the actual exaggeration in the way in which Bonhoeffer makes his point or of the pride in man's self-sufficiency that is expressed by Julian Huxley, but precisely in proceeding directly from Julian Huxley to Bonhoeffer he misses the connection—the actual connection—between sin and unhappiness.

The Biblical testimony concerning man is that he is an estranged creature ineluctably bound to his Creator in whose image he has been created and by whom he is eternally loved. The "image relation" is the Biblical category for saying that man is always man in responsive and responsible relation to God. "The Creator-creature" relation is the Biblical category for saying that in this human situation God remains Lord and takes the initiative to deal with man in his situation. "The Creator-creature" category is not a philosophical category. It is of the same dimension as the "sinner-Savior" category of which it is a correlate.

Bishop Robinson, in his discussion, deals with the fact of sin by using a quotation from Tillich.

> The state of our whole life is estrangement from others and ourselves, because we are estranged from the Ground of our being, because we are estranged from the origin and aim of our life. . . . We feel that something radical, total, and unconditioned is demanded of us; but we rebel against it, try to escape its urgency, and will not accept its promise.
> We cannot escape, however. If that something is the Ground of our being, we are bound to it for all eter-

nity, just as we are bound to ourselves and to all other life. We always remain in the power of that from which we are estranged. That fact brings us to the ultimate depth of sin.[4]

And then, speaking of grace, he says:

It happens; or it does not happen. And certainly it does *not* happen if we try to force it upon ourselves, just as it shall not happen so long as we think, in our self-complacency, that we have no need of it. Grace strikes us when we are in great pain and restlessness. It strikes us when we walk through the dark valley of a meaningless and empty life. It strikes us when we feel that our separation is deeper than usual, because we have violated another life, a life which we loved, or from which we were estranged. It strikes us when our disgust for our own being, our indifference, our weakness, our hostility, and our lack of direction and composure have become intolerable to us. It strikes us when, year after year, the longed-for perfection of life does not appear, when the old compulsions reign within us as they have for decades, when despair destroys all joy and courage. Sometimes at that moment a wave of light breaks into our darkness, and it is as though a voice were saying: "You are accepted. *You are accepted,* accepted by that which is greater than you, and the name of which you do not know."[5]

The inner connection between distress and despair cannot be spelled out more clearly, nor can the fact that the unhappiness of men is the unhappiness of sinners be brought out more forcibly.

But there is a different difficulty into which Tillich leads us. It can be plainly seen in the way in which Bishop Robinson puts the matter:

This new reality is transcendent, it is "beyond" us, in the sense that it is not ours to command. Yet we ex-

[4] Tillich, *The Shaking of the Foundations,* pp. 161 f.
[5] *Ibid.,* pp. 163 f.

perience it, like the Prodigal, as we "come to ourselves." For it is a coming home, or rather a being received home, to everything we are created to be. (HG, p. 80.)

"Grace strikes," "We are accepted," "We are received home"—but it is felt to be impermissible to talk of a God who is gracious, of a Savior who accepts, of a Father who receives us home. Even though in the statements made we, men, are the objects of the actions that take place, the effect of what is said lies in the claim that we have an experience of being struck by grace, that we have the experience of being accepted, that we have the experience of being received.

All this is true, but in the Bible it is consequential truth: it is consequential on the action and activity of God. It is not enough to say: "This new reality is transcendent, it is 'beyond' us, in the sense that it is not ours to command." It is beyond us in the much more simple sense that it is *from* beyond us.

Right through his book, Bishop Robinson makes the distinction between being which is ultimate and being which is not, between the eternal thou and the finite thou, between infinite depth and sinful surface, between creative ground and that which is grounded, between that which is of ultimate concern and that which is not. But these distinctions remain distinctions *within* man's self-knowledge, so that there is no way through to an apprehension of God as God. The situation is such that whatever man grasps becomes, in his grasp, man.

The whole point, on the other hand, of the Biblical way of speaking about sin is that the sinner finds not that he is constantly getting hold of himself at deeper and deeper levels, as Radhakrishnan puts it, but that he finds himself grasped more and more securely by God, to whom he belongs and by whose mercies he lives. The issue is not whether it is philosophically legitimate to talk about God as *a* being but whether it is possible to put into philosophically legitimate terms (and Bishop Robinson would say: the terms of ontology) the real crux of the Biblical message.

Bishop Robinson has been accused of denying that God is personal. It is an accusation easily refuted by his book. But where the Bishop fails to communicate the Christian message is where he fails to set out the Biblical announcement that God has acted on man's behalf. The whole trend of his argument is to make men realize the implications for their life of the fact that nothing can separate them from the love of God in Christ Jesus, but this love of God in Christ Jesus is conceived as a natural, though incredible, fact: a fact that is part of the structure of reality and is believed in because of that.

> To believe in God as love means to believe that in pure personal relationship we encounter, not merely what ought to be, but what is, the deepest, veriest truth about the structure of reality. This, in face of all the evidence, is a tremendous act of faith. But it is not the feat of persuading oneself of the existence of a super-Being beyond this world endowed with personal qualities. Belief in God is the trust, the well-nigh incredible trust, that to give ourselves to the uttermost in love is not to be confounded but to be "accepted," that Love is the ground of our being, to which ultimately we "come home." (HG, p. 49.)

> "There is nothing in death or life, . . . in the world as it is or the world as it shall be, in the forces of the universe, in heights or depths—nothing in all creation that can separate us from the love of God in Christ Jesus our Lord" (Rom. 8:38f., NEB). That I believe with all my being, and that is what at heart it means to be a Christian. As for the rest, as for the images of God, whether metal or mental, I am prepared to be an agnostic with the agnostic, even an atheist with the atheists. Such is the release I find in the story of St. Paul's great encounter with the men of Athens. (HG, p. 126–127.)

The reference here to Paul's speech at Athens is worth pursuing. What Bishop Robinson does with that speech is to draw the conclusion that Paul's attempt was to set the Athenians free from the worship of all idols so that they might worship the Unknown God. All that Paul wants to be sure about, the Bishop implies, is that they are brought to the conviction that ultimate reality is such that "nothing in all creation . . . can separate us from the love of God in Christ Jesus our Lord."

The actual incident at Athens surely points to a different method and motive and in a different direction. Paul fastens on four facts about man: he is religious, he is insecure, he is ignorant, he is God's offspring. (Paul uses here a term used by the Greek poets instead of the Hebrew term "image of God.") To this man, he says, you cannot therefore make images of God and worship them. Instead you must come to terms with what God himself has done: for this God who is Creator and whom you dimly feel after, this God who is the Giver and who is not dependent on anything that man does for him, this God who is Ruler and under whose decisions the peoples live, this God has announced his forgiveness of your ignorance, has commanded that you turn to him in repentance, has appointed for you a Judge and a Judgment and has done all these things by raising his appointed one from the dead (Acts 17:22–31).

The love of God in Christ is, indeed, part of the structure of reality, but one's conviction about it is not on the basis that it is part of the structure of reality but on the basis that one is able to accept it as part of the structure of reality because one's faith is held by those actions of God which made this so.

I would like to mention here an incident that happened at the Tambaram Conference of the International Missionary Council in the group that discussed the "Authority of the Faith." At one stage in the discussion

Henry P. Van Dusen, who was the chairman, asked some of the members present to express their Christian faith in three sentences. Kraemer defined it as follows: "I live by faith in the acts of God. I feel nothing about them. I stand on them." Walter Horton said, "I can put it into one sentence: I live by faith in the objective atonement of Christ." The force of both these definitions lies in the assertion that in God is the ground of our being because God has done something about it. He has made possible the overcoming of the distance between himself and man.

It is this testimony to the God who acts and has acted which is strangely absent from the book *Honest to God.* Even Bultmann, in whose writings the historical is dissolved in the existential, has this way of putting it:

> Man's life is moved by the search for God because it is always moved, consciously or unconsciously, by the question about his own personal existence. The question of God and the question of myself are identical. . . . In the fact that existentialist philosophy does not take into account the relation between man and God, the confession is implied that I cannot speak of God as my God by looking into myself. My personal relation with God can be made real by God only, by the acting God who meets me in His Word.[6]

It is not enough to say that ultimate reality is personal. It is essential, if one is to be true to the Biblical message, to communicate the faith that God acted on man's behalf. The problem of faith is not simply that of apprehending what God is but of responding to what God does. It is because this category of doing is so largely absent in the way Bishop Robinson presents his argument that his critics have contended that he denies the personality of God.

[6] Bultmann, *Jesus Christ and Mythology,* pp. 53, 59.

Let us now retrace our steps and go back to the summary of the mental picture of a God "out there" which we have already quoted from Bishop Robinson and which he desires to replace. (HG, p. 14.)

1. *The self-subsistence of the divine Being outside us and apart from us.*

The doctrine of the Trinity seeks to say that the personality of God is not unitary but societary. Community rather than individuality is the true hallmark of personality. But this Trinitarian doctrine which rests on the experience of the church in its worship of Father, Son, and Holy Spirit is not intended to assert, nor does it necessarily depend on, any conception of the self-subsistence of God outside us and apart from us.

When Paul uses the phrase "in him we live and move and have our being," he uses it to show that man's life is inextricably bound to the life of God. "We are his offspring." But the argument he builds on this is not that therefore man's search for God will be rewarded but that God's action on man's behalf is natural. The gospel is that God, whom men have worshiped and in whom they exist, has come to man in Jesus Christ. The issue is not concerning the self-subsistence of God but concerning God's activity: and, supremely, his action in the incarnation.

There is a statement by Bishop Robinson in which he introduces in parenthesis an explication, in the categories he prefers, of the doctrine of the Trinity. He says:

> In traditional theological terms, it was declaring that the way to "the Father"—to acknowledgement of the "ultimacy" of pure personal relationship —is only "by the Son"—through the love of him in whom the human is completely open to the divine—and "in the Spirit"— within the reconciling fellowship of the new community. (HG, p. 63.)

The parentheses are certainly true in themselves, but they do not touch the central concern enshrined in the doctrine of the Trinity. Let me state this concern in the lucid speech of Donald Baillie:

> What the doctrine of the Trinity really asserts is that it is God's very nature not only to create finite persons whom He could love, and to reveal and impart Himself to them, even to the point of incarnation (through His eternal Word) but also to extend this indwelling to those men who fail to obey Him, doing in them what they could not do themselves, supplying to them the obedience which He requires them to render (through His Holy Spirit). All of this, says the dogma of the Trinity, is of the eternal nature and essence of God. He is Father, Son and Holy Spirit, and the Son and the Spirit are consubstantial with the Father. And this outgoing love of God, His self-giving, is not new nor occasional nor transient, but "as it was in the beginning, is now, and ever shall be, world without end." Surely this doctrine is the objective expression of the same great paradox which finds its subjective expression in the confession: "Not I, but the grace of God."[7]

But lest the misunderstanding arise that by subjective expression Donald Baillie means talking about God in terms of subjective experience, let us look at the way in which he formulates this subjective expression. He is answering the question "What does the word 'God' mean in its true and full Christian use?"

> It means the One who at the same time makes absolute demands upon us and offers freely to give us all that He demands. It means the One who requires of us unlimited obedience and then supplies the obedience Himself. It means the One who calls us to work out our

[7] Donald Baillie, *God Was in Christ* (Charles Scribner's Sons, 1948; Faber & Faber, Ltd., London, 1956), pp. 122–123. Used with the permission of both publishers. Copyright 1948 Charles Scribner's Sons.

own salvation on the ground that "it is He Himself who works both the willing and the working" in our hearts and lives. It is not that He bestows His favour, His grace, upon those who render obedience to His commands. Such divine giving in response to human obedience is a sub-Christian idea, alien to the New Testament; and indeed if God's grace had to wait for man's obedience, it would be kept waiting for ever. But the Christian, when he has rendered his fullest and freest obedience, knows well that somehow it was "all of God," and he says: "It was not I, but the grace of God which was with me." This is the Creator-God who made us to be free personalities, and we know that we are most free and personal when He is most in possession of us. This is the God of the moral order who calls us every moment to exercise our full and responsible choice; but He also comes to dwell in us in such a way that we are raised altogether above the moral order into the liberty of the sons of God. That is what Christians mean by "God."[8]

Is Donald Baillie saying the same thing as Bishop Robinson? I believe he is, except that whereas the coordinates Baillie uses are God's gracious action and man's response, Robinson's coordinates are man's movement to his depth and man's discovery of grace. But it is this difference in the coordinates used which makes the final difference—the same set of coordinates will not serve to plot the graph of every equation—and this difference becomes explicit in Bishop Robinson's chapter on "Worldly Holiness." Together with much there that is truly and finely said, he finds it hardly necessary even to mention that relation between man and God which goes under the name of "adoration." He finds satisfying the position stated by John Wren-Lewis:

If the general atmosphere prevailing in a particular church is one which reverses the order of Jesus' state-

[8] *Ibid.*, p. 121.

ment, and conveys the sense that people actually go to church to *find* God, to enter into a relationship with him which is not possible apart from specific acts of worship, then it would be a miracle if you *did* get the right thing out of going to such a church, and one has no business tempting God by asking for miracles. It is *much* better to stay away. (HG, p. 90.)

The fact still remains that while men and women do not go to church to find God because he cannot be found elsewhere or in other ways, they do go to church to express a relation with him that is not possible (except in exceptional circumstances) apart from specific acts of worship. The predicament of refusing any meaning to God "out there" is to get shut up with oneself and so be shut up in the poetry of personal religion in however secular a form that religion may be practiced and in however secular a terminology it may be expounded.

2. *The creation of the world by God and its existence over against him.*

When one says that God is love, the word "love" is adjectival in intent. It really means that God is loving. When one says, on the other hand, that God is the ground of our being, the meaning seems to be that the ground of our being is God. But we cannot say this, even as we cannot say that love is God. God is known as the ground of our being. God is knowable because in him is the ground of our being. God maintains his relation to us as the ground of our being. It is an activity of God on which the primary assertion depends. This is what the doctrine of creation asserts. The issue is not about the moment of time when creation came into being but about the relationship between the world and God—a relationship of creature and Creator. As Donald Baillie remarks:

In contrast to every theory of temporal origins, it [the doctrine of Creation] probably involves the idea that time itself is part of creation, and this again is highly paradoxical. Yet these paradoxes are inescapable. Theology is driven to them. Moreover, it is Christian theology in particular that is driven to them. It is, we may say, in the endeavour to think out the religion of the Incarnation that the human mind has been led even to the paradoxes of Creation—to the peculiarly Christian and wholly paradoxical doctrine of creatio ex nihilo.[9]

Creatio ex nihilo is certainly a paradox, but it is a necessary paradox that points to the distinction between Creator and creature.

In the statement that God calls the world into existence over against himself, exception may be taken to the idea that God is a being over against whom the world exists, but the category of depth being inadequate to express the creaturely existence of the world, the category of "over-against-ness" is used.

It is true that the doctrine of creation has often been misstated. Instead of pointing to God and his relation to the world, it has been made to point to the world and its origin in time. As Reinhold Niebuhr puts it:

> Thus the idea of the divine creation of the world, which, when taken profoundly, describes the limits of the world's rationality and the inadequacy of any "natural" cause as a sufficient explanation for the irrational givenness of things, is frequently corrupted into a theory of secondary causation and thereby comes in conflict with a valid scientific account of causation on the natural level. This corruption of religion into a bad science has aroused the justified protest of a scientific age. It also helped to tempt science to become a bad religion by offering natural causation as an adequate principle of ultimate coherence.[10]

[9] *Ibid.*, p. 111.

[10] Reinhold Niebuhr, *Faith and History* (Charles Scribner's Sons, 1949; James Nisbet & Co., Ltd., London, 1949), p. 37. Used with the permission of Charles Scribner's Sons.

But perhaps the real difficulty in all this lies in our inability to talk of God doing anything because we are told that we must not think of him or speak of him as *a* being. Does not the answer to this difficulty lie not in jettisoning the Biblical category of "the Living God"—the God who acts—but in remembering that with all its paradox "God" in the Bible has the force of a proper name.

> The word "God," rightly understood, [says Donald Baillie] is not a common noun but a proper name. That is why Brunner makes the idea of the "name of God" so important in his theology, and conceives of revelation as "God telling us His name," on the basis of the story of Moses and the burning bush, and many other biblical passages. And yet this is not like any other proper name. It does not indicate particularity, one instance of a class, for God is not in any class. Common names, say the logicians, possess connotation, but proper names possess only denotation. May it not be said, however, that "God" is the one proper name that does possess connotation? And yet it is a connotation that cannot be fully conceptualized. Its meaning cannot be expressed without paradox.[11]

It is thus that the Biblical affirmation of God as creator carries with it the double implication that man is related to him as worshiper and as him to whom God speaks. When psalmist and prophet insist that man's maker is his God, they are insisting that men must not worship that which they themselves have created. "You shall not make yourself a graven image." (Ex. 20:4.) It would be an interesting development when all images of God, metal and mental, are destroyed and then men turn in worship to the depths of their own being. It is only a superficial criticism of the images of "height" and "distance" when

[11] Donald Baillie, *op. cit.,* p. 119.

these are made to speak of God's unconcern (HG, p. 46).
The ministry of these images to the spirit of man is that
they lead him to the act of worship. But in worship, the
distance is known to be bridged because man finds himself not only worshiping God but being addressed by him.

> O come, let us worship and bow down,
>   let us kneel before the Lord, *our Maker!*
> For he is our God,
>   and we are the people of his pasture,
>   and the sheep of his hand.
> *O that today you would hearken to his voice!*
> (Ps. 95:6–7.)

It is this double situation that the Bible speaks about
when it speaks about the covenanting God.

3. *God as he covenants himself with men.*

This is the third element in the picture of "God out
there" that Bishop Robinson lists in his summary of traditional theology.

What is the Biblical concern in its witness to God as
the covenanting God? It is, in the first place, to insist
that creation is not "past tense." In the words of Tillich:

The doctrine of creation is not the story of an event
which took place "once upon a time." It is the basic
description of the relation between God and the world.
It is the correlate to the analysis of man's finitude. It
answers the question implied in man's finitude and in
finitude generally. In giving this answer it discovers that
the meaning of finitude is creatureliness. The doctrine
of creation is the answer to the question implied in the
creature as creature. This question is asked continually
and is always answered in man's essential nature. The
question and the answer are beyond potentiality and
actuality, as all things are in the process of the divine
life. But actually the question is asked and is not answered in man's existential situation. The character of

existence is that man asks the question of his finitude without receiving an answer. It follows that even if there were such a thing as natural theology, it could not reach the truth of God's creativity and man's crea- tureliness. The doctrine of creation does not describe an event. It points to the situation of creatureliness and to its correlate, the divine creativity.[12]

In the second place, it is to insist that this continuing creativity of God is neither seen nor known nor under- stood apart from the fact that a people were pulled up short by him. The uniqueness of Israel's conviction as the chosen people lies in their affirmation that they did not choose God but that God chose them, and that for this choice no reason can be given.

It was not because you were more in number than any other people that the Lord set his love upon you and chose you, for you were the fewest of all peoples; but it is because the Lord loves you, and is keeping the oath which he swore to your fathers, that the Lord has brought you out with a mighty hand, and redeemed you from the house of bondage, from the hand of Pharaoh king of Egypt. (Deut. 7:7–8.)

Both Reinhold Niebuhr and Herbert Butterfield make the same point in describing this peculiar quality in Is- rael's sense of its choice.

The idea of God choosing Israel as an act of grace, since Israel had no power or virtue to merit the choice, represents a radical break in the history of culture. It is, in a genuine sense, the beginning of revelation; for here a nation apprehends and is apprehended by the true God and not by a divine creature of its own contrivance. The proof of the genuineness of His Majesty and the

[12] Paul Tillich, *Systematic Theology, Vol. I* (The University of Chicago Press, 1951; James Nisbet & Co., Ltd., London, 1953), pp. 280–281. Used with the permission of The University of Chicago Press. Copyright 1951 by The University of Chicago.

truth of His Divinity is attested by the fact that He confronts the nation and the individual as the limit, and not the extension, of its own power and purpose.[13]

What was unique about the ancient Hebrews was their historiography rather than their history—the fact that their finer spirits saw the hand of God in events, ultimately realising that if they were the Chosen People they were chosen for the purpose of transmitting that discovery to all the other nations. Their historiography was unique also in that it ascribed the successes of Israel not to virtue but to the favour of God; and instead of narrating the glories or demonstrating the righteousness of the nation, like our modern patriotic histories, it denounced the infidelity of the people, denounced it not as an occasional thing but as the constant feature of the nation's conduct throughout the centuries; even proclaiming at times that the sins of Israel were worse, and their hearts more hardened against the light, than those of the other nations around them.[14]

So follows the third insistence of the Biblical testimony that God's covenant with Israel points beyond Israel to God's covenant with all men.

The rigour of the prophetic conception of the divine transcendence, [says Reinhold Niebuhr] contributes to the idea of a universal history in two ways: First history is conceived as a unity because all historical destinies are under the dominion of a single divine sovereignty. (Amos 9:7.) The second contribution is contained in the rigour with which the inclination of every human collective, whether tribe, nation or empire, to make itself the centre of universal history, is overcome in principle.[15]

[13] Niebuhr, *Faith and History*, p. 117.
[14] Herbert Butterfield, *Christianity and History* (Charles Scribner's Sons, 1950; G. Bell & Sons, Ltd., London, 1949), p. 73.
[15] Niebuhr, *Faith and History*, pp. 120, 128.

The issue concerning "transcendence" then cannot be settled by arguing away "God out there"; it has to reckon, in the final analysis, with the Biblical insistence that God is God transcendent over human history. It is not enough simply to ground all history in God and see there the basis of man's hope; it is essential that this ground be known and its contours drawn in historical terms. That is why the category of "covenant" as describing God's relation to man and his history is more satisfying than the inclusive category of self-transcendence.

Again, what is at stake is that men fall down and worship. God our Maker is also the God of our fathers. Their history is the context of meaning in which we stand. To the cry of the psalmist: "We have heard with our ears, O God, our fathers have told us, what deeds thou didst perform in their days, in the days of old" (Ps. 44:1), there is a reply: "We have this as a sure and steadfast anchor of the soul, a hope that enters into the inner shrine behind the curtain, where Jesus has gone as a forerunner on our behalf" (Heb. 6:19–20).

4. *The Son who came and must come again.*

The quotation from The Letter to the Hebrews, which we have just seen, gives us here our starting point. "Jesus has gone as a forerunner on our behalf, having become a high priest for ever after the order of Melchizedek." Here there is a frank recognition of "coming" and "going," together with the assertion that Jesus is after the order of Melchizedek that is "without father or mother or genealogy, and has neither beginning of days nor end of life" (Heb. 7:3). The striking thing about this passage is that the name used is "Jesus"—the specific human being, Jesus of Nazareth.

What Bishop Robinson finds difficult in all this language about coming and going is that there is, according to him, nowhere to come from and nowhere to go to. But the Biblical witness is not about a whence or whither but about a from whom and to whom. "Jesus, knowing . . . that he had come from God and was going to God . . ." (John 13:3.) "I came from the Father and have come into the world; again, I am leaving the world and going to the Father." (John 16:28.)

> In St. John [says Archbishop Ramsey] there is again and again that "deep down" apprehension which has been one of the secrets of his power to elicit the sense of God in many generations. But is it possible to tear apart the "deep down" realization and the imagery of the Beyond, of heaven, of coming and going, which is part of the fabric of the story?
>
> It is in the imagery of that dimension that we see the depth of the divine humility, the humility of Bethlehem as well as of the feet-washing and Calvary.[16]

The specific reason given by the writer of The Letter to the Hebrews for talking about Jesus in this way is that he has neither beginning nor end. He is the Eternal One within time. It is significant that the only other figure to whom Jesus is compared in the New Testament is Adam. This means that the paradox which the New Testament is conscious of in thus talking about Jesus is the paradox of time. The spatial connotation of "from" and "to" is not present at all. What is the paradox of time? In its simplest terms, it consists in the assertion that what happened in the Christ event was always true of covenanted God and yet that in the Christ event something happened and was not simply manifested.

The quality of eternity in the Christ event is expressed with great clarity by Donald Baillie. He says:

> To reduce the importance of the historical event would be contrary to every instinct of the Christian faith; and yet it seems impossible to say that the divine sin-bearing

16 Ramsey, *op. cit.,* p. 10.

was confined to that moment of time, or is anything
less than eternal. . . . As God was incarnate in Jesus,
so we may say that the divine Atonement was incarnate
in the passion of Jesus. And if we then go on to speak
of an eternal Atonement in the very life and being of
God, it is not by way of reducing the significance of the
historical moment of the Incarnation, but by way of
realizing the relation of the living God to every historical moment. God's reconciling work cannot be confined to any one moment of history. We cannot say that
God was unforgiving until Christ came and died on
Calvary; nor can we forget that God's work of reconciliation still goes on in every age in the lives of sinful
men, whose sins He still bears.[17]

On the other hand, the crucial quality of happening in
the Christ event finds equally lucid expression by him:

And if we say, with the voice of the Christian ages, that
Jesus died for sinners, it will be well for us to realize
at the outset that this is profoundly true, not merely
as a matter of theological interpretation, concerning the
overruling purpose of God, but also in a purely historical sense, in respect of Jesus' personal relations with
the sinners in ancient Galilee. . . .

Quite apart from . . . all subsequent theological inter-
pretations, it is true in the plainest historical sense that
Jesus died for sinners: it was His love for them that
brought Him to the Cross. . . .

The crucifixion of Jesus set men thinking more than
anything else that has ever happened in the life of the
human race. And the most remarkable fact in the whole
history of religious thought is this: that when the early
Christians looked back and pondered on the dreadful
thing that had happened, it made them think of the re-
deeming love of God.

Not simply of the love of Jesus, but of the love of God.[18]

[17] Donald Baillie, *op. cit.*, pp. 190, 191.
[18] *Ibid.*, pp. 181, 183–184.

Does it not seem that what the New Testament is seeking to do is to speak to a man as he is confronted by the divine forgiveness and tell him: Look at that person— Jesus. He is the Christ. This is how it happened. This is what it means. This is it. So that, as the New Testament witness is heard, men experience the crashing into their own lives of an event that actually happened long ago and that lifts them into the eternal life of God from where that event proceeded and to where it returns with humanity in its train.

> Was it not then [says John Baillie] a gracious ordering of things on God's part that there should be ultimate salvation for us all in only one Name; that we can meet with him only by meeting with one another; by betaking ourselves all together to one place—to one "green hill far away"; by encountering there a single Figure to whom we offer our united allegiance; by listening to the self-same story; by reading in the same sacred book; by being baptized into the same fellowship; by eating and drinking at the same Holy Table; so that "there is no difference between Jew and Greek, for the same Lord is Lord of all," and "here there is not Greek and Jew, circumcised and uncircumcised, barbarian, Scythian, slave, or free man, but Christ is all and in all." Is it not true that we cannot have real unity until we all have "the same Lord"?[19]

The purpose of this chapter thus far has been to look at the basic themes of traditional Christian theology that Bishop Robinson himself has mentioned and question whether they can be stated compellingly in the kind of terminology which the Bishop thinks is the only terminology which many in our time will accept.

But before closing this chapter, I would like us to look at what our Lord himself taught us. He said, "When you pray, say: Father, . . . Thy kingdom come." Prayer is the

[19] John Baillie, *The Sense of the Presence of God*, p. 209.

true posture in which to think about God;[20] and here, in response to the disciples' request that he teach them to pray, Jesus tells them, when you pray address God as Father, also think of him as King.

Here are two images. What do we say of them? It is Tillich's contention that

> Any concrete assertion about God must be symbolic, for a concrete assertion is one which uses a segment of finite experience in order to say something about him.
>
> Can a segment of finite reality become the basis for an assertion about that which is infinite? The answer is that it can, because that which is infinite is being-itself and because everything participates in being-itself. . . . The *analogia entis* gives us our only justification of speaking at all about God. It is based on the fact that God must be understood as being-itself.[21]

John Baillie contests this position of Tillich. How can we say that this is nearer to perfection than that unless we already have some conception of what perfection is?

> What is true [he says] in the doctrine of the *analogia entis* is that the knowledge of God does not precede our knowledge of man in time but is given "in, with and under" such knowledge, and that therefore no one of

---

[20] Compare the following statement by J. H. Oldham in *Life Is Commitment,* p. 47: "God is not an object among other objects. He is not a cause among other causes. He is not, as we tend to think of Him, an immensely great and powerful person alongside of other persons. All these ways of thinking of Him make Him part of the world. God cannot be part of the world; He is the creator and sustainer of the world. He does not belong to the objective world at all. When we objectify Him, He ceases to be God. We have set up an idol in His place. . . . It is true that we cannot, in fact, think or speak of God without objectifying Him. That means that, strictly speaking, we cannot talk about God. We can only talk to Him. *Where God is concerned the only language open to us is prayer.*"

[21] Tillich, *Systematic Theology,* Vol. I, pp. 265, 266.

God's attributes is ever given us save in conjunction with—that is, in comparison with and in contrast to—some corresponding attribute of man. What is false is the assumption that the comparison moves from man to God instead of from God to man.[22]

We cannot [he quotes] reach the Divine merely by way of inference, not even if the inference be analogical in character. By no idealization of the creaturely can we transcend the creaturely.[23]

And then referring directly to the use of the name "Father" for God, John Baillie quotes Karl Barth.

It must not be said that the name "Father" for God is a transference to God, figurative and not to be taken literally, of a human creaturely relationship, whereas God's essential being as God *per se* is not touched or characterized by this name. . . . But what is figurative and not literal is that which we characterize and imagine we know as fatherhood in our human creaturely sphere.[24]

If the Creative is the standard of the propriety of the created, and therefore also of our language, then the reverse is true. . . . *God alone . . . as He who is by Himself, as the eternal Father of the eternal Son, is properly and adequately to be called Father.*[25]

John Baillie concludes:

Not all who are in the bare factual sense fathers display the character of fatherliness even in a minimal degree. Only God possesses it and displays it in per-

[22] John Baillie, *Our Knowledge of God* (Charles Scribner's Sons, 1939; Oxford University Press, 1939), p. 254.

[23] Kemp Smith, *Is Divine Existence Credible?* (Oxford University Press, 1931), p. 14.

[24] Karl Barth, *Credo* (Charles Scribner's Sons, 1962; Hodder & Stoughton, Ltd., London, 1935), pp. 23 f.

[25] Karl Barth, *Church Dogmatics*, Vol. I, Part 1 (T. & T. Clark, Edinburgh, 1936), pp. 413 f.

fection; and it is only by the standard of his perfect
fatherliness that we can measure the appropriateness
of the attribution of fatherliness to any man. So far,
then, Dr. Barth speaks truly when he says that God
alone is properly and adequately to be called Father,
and that *it is in no figurative sense that we so call him.*
The divine is always prior. The ideal is always a priori.
Only if something of its nature is revealed to us, can
we proceed to the grading or valuation of the actual.

At all events it is certain that Christians have always
believed that such knowledge as they can have of God
is the fruit of a divine initiative whereby God seeks to
make himself known. The faith of which it has spoken
has always been conceived as a response to the divine
approach. It is the apprehension of a divine communication.[26]

In other words, when Jesus told us to call God
"Father," he meant that that is what God is: He is "the
Father, from whom every family in heaven and on earth
is named" (Eph. 3:14–15) and that this apprehension
of God is distinguished from other forms of apprehension because only through Him (Jesus) was this
apprehension possible. "No one comes to the Father, but
by me." (John 14:6.)

In God as Father is certainly the ground of our being,
but this is neither symbol nor analogy, it is the acknowledgment of the relation that God maintains between himself and men. "The God who does" is rightly called
"Father." The Fatherhood of God is such that his children
are able to live in complete dependence on him, upheld
by his love, surrounded by his goodness, trusting in his
faithfulness, and bound to one another by his common
love for them all. The relation is a dynamic one in which
the action and activity of God are determinative.

[26] John Baillie, *The Sense of the Presence of God*, pp. 121,
125.

The same dynamism is present in the use of the word "King." The reign of the King is the ground of being of his citizens. The citizens are upheld by his rule, their lives are determined by the laws he promulgates, their work is directed by his purposes and policies, and their sins are dealt with according to his judgment. It just will not do to take these consequences of God's fatherhood and God's reign and make them descriptive of the nature of human existence at its depths, without in some way recognizing that these are consequences of what God himself is and does.

The point of departure for any true speaking of God, then, does not lie either in man's capacity or incapacity to seek the infinite, in man's ability to reach into the depths or to proceed by analogy to the heights, but on the foundation fact to which the Bible bears persistent testimony that "God does not forsake the work of his hands."

> The Lord will fulfil his purpose for me;
>   thy steadfast love, O Lord, endures for ever.
> Do not forsake the work of thy hands.
>   (Ps. 138:8.)

In holding to the way of speech that Jesus taught us, therefore, we are taking our stand on high ground. We are not simply saying that we prefer to use the language he taught rather than the language which Bishop Robinson or Professor Tillich will have us use. We are saying, rather, that it is in the words which Jesus taught that there is established both man's true relation to God and true witness is borne to him in human speech.

Indeed, the protest against thinking about God as *a* Being can go too far. It can make impossible an understanding of God as he works and of his works. A thoroughgoing use of the concept of God as simply the ground of all being will lead to an understanding of history in which nothing happens. Things appear and disappear, there is

change and becoming, there is flux but there is no movement to a destination. I cannot help recalling the comment of a Hindu friend of mine who, after reading
Tillich, said to me, "This is bad Hinduism."

Bishop Robinson, again and again, makes the point
that supranaturalism as a category of thought is unaccept-
able. He agrees with the call of Bultmann to abandon
the entire conception of a supernatural order which in-
vades and perforates this one. As Tillich puts it:

> To criticise such a conditioning of the unconditional,
> even if it leads to atheistic consequences, is more re-
> ligious, because it is more aware of the unconditional
> character of the divine, than a theism that bans God
> into the supranatural realm.[27]

But the position of those who speak of the supernatural,
or supranatural, is not understood unless it is seen that
the quality of ultimacy which belongs to the depths of
personal existence and interpersonal relationships is, for
them, a quality that is not natural to natural order but
belongs to the natural order as an act of grace. If Tillich
is right that, within itself, the finite world points beyond
itself, then that to which it points exists within itself as
having come from beyond. The quotation from Martin
Buber in which he, speaking of a person who professedly
denies God, says:

> When he, too, who abhors the name, and believes him-
> self to be godless, gives his whole being to addressing
> the Thou of his life, as a Thou that cannot be limited
> by another, he addresses God—[28]

testifies to two things: that the unconditional exists in the
conditioned and that the conditioned recognizes this as a

[27] Paul Tillich, *The Protestant Era* (The University of Chicago Press, 1948; James Nisbet & Co., Ltd., London, 1951),
p. 92.

[28] Martin Buber, *I and Thou,* 2d ed. (Charles Scribner's Sons,
1958; T. & T. Clark, Edinburgh, 1937), p. 76.

Thou. Here again the Thou who is recognized is recognized as Being himself, whereas I am a being.

The point at issue, in the last analysis, is how to state the transcendence of God in such a way as to make sense of the fundamental claim of the Bible, that the Christian message lies in what God has done to deal with the sinfulness of man and the sin in which all creation is involved. As the book *Honest to God* shows, the meaning of transcendence can be stated in such a way as to make unnecessary the thought of God as a personal being wholly other to man, dwelling in majesty. But this book also shows that this way of speaking of God's transcendence is inadequate to set out either the radical nature of sin or the decisive nature of God's act in Christ. The sieve through which the Christian message has been passed has not allowed its essential nature to come through. The battle in the New Testament, and the battle ever since, has not been about mere meanings but about the meaning of events. To a consideration of the great event in Jesus of Nazareth we must now turn.

4

The Man Christ Jesus

W E LOVE HIM who first loved us, and the Bible does not anywhere try to convince us that the word love means two completely different things in the two references. Analogy may be applied to the logic of our propositions so that we can at least see what is meant by those who seek to distinguish what is applicable from that which is not applicable to God. But there is no comparable concept available for the division of our emotions and affections. Here we are bound to our anthropomorphism, even when we seek the very highest object for our love and devotion. . . . If, therefore, in our interpretation of love as concern, we find that we are committed to what by the standards of scholasticism may appear to be anthropomorphic ways of thought and expression, we take courage and justification from the devotional situation into which the Bible leads us—the presence of a God Who has made us His concern and Who calls now for the living response of wills conformable to His. For at the very heart of the Bible where we meet God in devotion there stands the *man* that was called Jesus, and from that "Anthropos" no proper theology can ever hope to escape.[1]

But it is just here that a reader of the New Testament is presented with his chief problem. He is told on so

[1] McIntyre, *op. cit.*, pp. 61–62.

many hands that, while an actual man—Jesus—did live, it is not possible to know very much about him and that, in any case, this failure to know does not much matter. What matters is that there came into existence a community of people who had been led to say: In Jesus, the midpoint of history has been reached; the climactic intervention of God in the affairs of men has been made; man's experience of God has become direct; the reconciliation of humanity with God has been effected.

In faith we are not concerned with the Jesus of history as historical science sees Him, but with the Jesus Christ of personal testimony, who is the real Christ, and whom John shows just as plainly as the Synoptists. . . . Faith presupposes, as a matter of course, a priori, that the Jesus of history is not the same as the Christ of faith.[2]

The idea that faith is in any sense based on the impression made by the personality of Jesus is completely mistaken. The New Testament has no interest in the "personality" of Jesus, nor in any "personality," for that very word indicates an attitude and outlook that are alien to Christianity. . . . It is impossible from the study of the Gospels (which were never meant for such a purpose) to discover what Jesus was like as a human personality; and because, even if we could discover it, the result would be disappointing to those who expected to find a revelation there, since only a "divine incognito," a veiling of God, was present in the human life of Jesus.[3]

Interest in the personality of Jesus is excluded, and not merely because, in the absence of information, I am making a virtue of necessity. I do indeed think that we

[2] Emil Brunner, *The Mediator* (The Westminster Press, 1947; Lutterworth Press, London, 1934), pp. 159, 184.

[3] Karl Barth, *The Doctrine of God,* pp. 126, 453. (See also summary of Barth's position on p. 37 of Donald Baillie's *God Was in Christ.*)

can now know almost nothing concerning the life and personality of Jesus, since the early Christian sources show no interest in either, and are, moreover, fragmentary and often legendary, and other sources about Jesus do not exist. . . . For whose interest is in the personality of Jesus this situation is depressing or destructive; for our purpose it has no particular significance.[4]

It seems, then, that the form of the earthly no less than of the heavenly Christ is for the most part hidden from us. . . . And perhaps the more we ponder the matter, the more clearly we shall understand the reason for it, and therefore shall not wish it otherwise. For probably we are as little prepared for the one as for the other.[5]

The reports about Jesus of Nazareth are those of Jesus as the Christ, given by persons who had received him as the Christ. Therefore, if one tries to find the real Jesus behind the picture of Jesus as the Christ, it is necessary critically to separate the elements which belong to the factual side of the event from the elements which belong to the receiving side. In doing so, one sketches a "Life of Jesus"; and innumerable such sketches have been made. . . . But none can claim to be a probable picture which is the result of the tremendous scientific toil dedicated to this task for two hundred years. At best, they are more or less probable results, able to be the basis neither of an acceptance nor of a rejection of the Christian faith.[6]

Knowledge of revelation, although it is mediated primarily through historical events, does not imply factual assertions, and it is therefore not exposed to critical analysis by historical research. Its truth is to be judged

[4] Rudolf Bultmann, *Jesus and the Word* (Charles Scribner's Sons, n. d.; Nicholson & Watson, Ltd., London, 1935), pp. 8 f., 13 f.

[5] R. H. Lightfoot, *History and Interpretation in the Gospels* (Harper & Row, Publishers, Inc., 1935; Hodder & Stoughton, Ltd., London, 1935), *ad fin.*

[6] Tillich, *Systematic Theology*, Vol. II, p. 118.

by criteria which lie within the dimension of revelatory knowledge.[7]

There is one direction in which all these statements point that is of real importance. Men come to faith not through a knowledge of the life of Jesus as it was lived in Palestine but through the impact of the New Testament witness to Jesus repeated and reinforced by the witness to him of the Christian community across the generations. Reinhold Niebuhr makes the following point:

> There is significantly no hint in the Gospel record of any gradual understanding even in the inner circle of disciples of the true meaning of Christ's death. Peter's confession of his Master's messianic ministry was immediately followed by a rejection of the tragic culmination of it which Christ predicted. In the Lukan account of Christ's appearance to his disciples at Emmaus they remain oblivious of the real meaning of his life, ruefully confessing, "We trusted that it had been he who would have redeemed Israel" (Luke 24:21). The church is thus not grounded upon a slowly dawning consciousness of the true significance of Christ. It is founded in the miracle of the recognition of the true Christ in the resurrection.[8]

This means that the way to faith in Jesus Christ, even today, is not a slowly dawning consciousness of who he is, produced by a meditation on his life as it was lived, but rather it is a crashing conviction wrought by personal confrontation with the risen Christ, a confrontation mediated within the ongoing life and testimony of the Christian community.

But it is impossible that this should be so unless there is true congruence between the life of Jesus as it was lived in Palestine and the frame of faith within which that life has come to be understood and set out. The need

[7] Tillich, *Systematic Theology*, Vol. I, p. 144.
[8] Niebuhr, *Faith and History*, p. 167.

is that the portrait of Christ which lies behind the
church's confession of him should be reliable, and not
that we should be able to go behind the portrait and ob-
tain a photograph.

> Faith alone is able to know rightly the historical reality
> of Jesus Christ.[9]

> It is true in a sense that the science of history cannot
> directly introduce the supramundane and the divine
> into its nexus of causes and effects, cannot penetrate
> into a supra-historical "dimension." In that sense the
> "historical" is the "human"; the sphere of history is the
> life of man, the dimension of humanity. But even then,
> are we to forget that the humanity of our Lord is vital
> to Christian faith? And can even His humanity be
> worthily studied without the sympathy and insight of
> faith? Without this, surely the historical study of such
> a subject would be vain. It would not be soundly his-
> torical. The result would be bad history. It would not
> give us Jesus as He really was. It would not give us the
> Jesus of history.[10]

> On what is our Christian faith based? If we cannot
> validly find any revelation of God in the portrait of
> Jesus as an historical person, how are we ever to reach
> and accept the dogmas about Him? If we cannot get so
> far as to know what He was like, or if that has nothing
> to do with the real meaning of the story, then how can
> we go so much farther and know that God was in-
> carnate in Him?[11]

> The name Jesus Christ is not the transparent shell,
> through which we glimpse something higher—no room
> for Platonism here! What is involved is this actual
> name and this title; this person is involved.[12]

[9] Brunner, *op. cit.*, p. 162.
[10] Donald Baillie, *op. cit.*, pp. 47–48.
[11] *Ibid.*, p. 50.
[12] Karl Barth, *Dogmatics in Outline* (Alec R. Allenson, Inc.,
1955; SCM Press, Ltd., London, 1949), p. 67.

But this inward testimony can find nothing to feed upon if we are presented with a bare name and not at the same time told anything about the Person whose name it is.[13]

But can we know the Jesus of history? A discussion of this subject would take us beyond the scope of this book. Suffice it to say that the present position in New Testament studies is strong ground for hope that we are again at the threshold of a new understanding and knowledge of Jesus as he was.[14] How indispensable such a knowledge is, was challengingly stated by Dr. W. D. Davies in his Inaugural Lecture when he was inducted as professor of Biblical theology at Union Theological Seminary, New York. Speaking on the subject "A Quest [the quest for the historical Jesus] to Be Resumed in New Testament Studies," he said:

[13] John Baillie, *The Sense of the Presence of God,* p. 191.

[14] Here is a statement of a conservative position on this question by an acknowledged authority on New Testament studies: "The connection of events ceases to be 'accidental' if the tradition as we can recover it from the New Testament represents in substance a true memory of the facts, with the meaning which they really bore as an episode in history. We cannot, however, prove that this is so. What we can hope to prove is that in the fourth decade of the first century the Christian Church grew up around a central tradition which, however it is expressed—in preaching, in story, in teaching and in liturgical practice— yields a coherent picture of Jesus Christ, what He was, what He stood for, what He said, did and suffered. The step beyond that will probably be taken by something more akin to faith than to objective historical judgment. Either the interpretation through which the facts are presented was imposed upon them mistakenly —and in that case few facts remain which we can regard as strictly ascertained—or the interpretation was imposed by the facts themselves, as they were experienced in an historical situation, and gave rise to historical consequences—and in that case we do know, in the main, what the facts were. The latter conclusion may not be demonstrable, but it is not unreasonable." (C. H. Dodd, *History and the Gospel* [Charles Scribner's Sons, 1938; James Nisbet & Co., Ltd., London, 1938], pp. 109–110.)

As long as the Jesus of History was a significant factor in the interpretation of the Faith of the New Testament, the works and words of Jesus themselves provided a content for the Kerygma which was religiously and ethically enriching. But once the Kerygma was materially divorced from these, it could not but become to some extent an empty shell, or, as I have before expressed it, a skeleton with no flesh. And it is of the nature of skeletons that they call for explanation. This is, in part, the reason for the urgency with which Bultmann has called for demythologizing. When the Kerygma had become mainly a bare divine action from beyond that touched earth only at the point of the Cross, its mythological character became markedly prominent at the expense of its historical substance, and so Bultmann came to explain the mythology not so much in terms of its historical content as of his own philosophic presuppositions. Exegesis, no less than nature, abhors a vacuum. The neglect of the historical Jesus left the house of the Kerygma empty for the entry of things other than the works and words of Jesus.[15]

This denouement in the West is debilitating; for those of us who live under the shadow of Hinduism and Buddhism in the East it is disastrous. (Of course, if the proposition is true in itself that the Jesus of history cannot be known, then Christianity in the East will have to accept that disaster: but is it true?) At a Hindu-Christian colloquium held at Kerala (India), one of the Hindu participants made the following characteristic statement: "It is possible for a Hindu to have Krishna or Christ, Siva or

Dr. Davies himself adopts a more expectant attitude than his teacher, Dr. Dodd: in support of which he quotes particularly the work of Prof. Harold Riesenfeld and his brilliant thesis, expounded at the International Congress on the Gospels held at Oxford in 1957.

[15] W. D. Davies, *Christian Origins and Judaism* (The Westminster Press, 1962; Darton, Longman & Todd, Ltd., London, 1961), p. 9.

Allah as his chosen Deity. Every faith is only an aspect of the Eternal Religion."[16]

The point of interest in this statement is that Christ is ranged alongside the various names of deity. The speaker is not thinking of Jesus of Nazareth. Why should he, if Jesus of Nazareth is only a name, only a point of reference! The full force of the contention, therefore, must be maintained that, in speaking of Jesus the Christ, we are talking about an actual person—what he said and what he did and what happened to him.

> All four Gospels [says Prof. Charles Moule, of Cambridge] are alike to be interpreted as more than anything else evangelistic and apologetic in purpose, and that the Synoptic Gospels represent primarily the recognition that a vital element in evangelism is the plain story of what happened in the ministry of Jesus.[17]

> I will merely state [concludes Dr. Davies in the lecture we have already quoted] in theological justification of the position I have been advocating, that it would seem to me essential that there should be no incongruity between the Jesus of History and the Christ of Faith. The problem of their congruity cannot be silenced or shelved. Should they be incongruous, while a Theology of the Word might be possible, a Theology of the Word made flesh would hardly be so, and it is to such a Theology that the New Testament commits us.[18]

A different but supplementary discussion of this question has taken place in which the approach was not from the side of historical studies of the New Testament but from the side of theology itself. If it could be shown that, in its doctrine of incarnation, what the New Testament is really saying is that the universal became particular,

[16] *Religion and Society,* September, 1962, p. 34.
[17] *New Testament Essays—Studies in Memory of T. W. Manson* (Manchester University Press, Manchester, 1959), pp. 175 f.
[18] Davies, *op. cit.,* p. 17.

then we can let the particular simply point to the universal
and so concentrate our attention on the universal itself.
This is the tendency of Tillich's thought. In discussing
such a tendency, Kraemer makes clear where the real
issue lies. He says:

> In his philosophical language Tillich defines the
> incarnation by the words: "das Wesen ist in die
> Erscheinung getreten" (i.e., the Essence, Being has ap-
> peared on the plane of appearance). This philosophical
> way of speaking in itself is inadequate to the faithful
> interpretation of John 1. The soteriological aim of the
> Johannine Logos doctrine would be a corpus alienum
> to the ontological Universal Logos. The main question
> is: does not a faithful interpretation of John 1 imply
> that the manifestation of the "concrete Logos become
> flesh" in Jesus necessarily means a judgment on all
> thinking, proceeding from obedience to the Universal
> Logos? It certainly does, if we remind ourselves of
> John 1:5, 10, 11. Tillich virtually as well as explicitly
> denies this.[19]

In this connection, Kraemer brings under criticism also
the exegesis of the Johannine prologue by Bultmann.
Whereas Tillich makes the Logos concept neutralize the
human particular, Bultmann will not allow the particular
to be the content of the Logos. He interprets the Johannine prologue as a redemption myth and seeks "to prove
that the gospel about Jesus the Saviour, as it is expressed
in the Logos passage of John, is a gnostic myth, fastened
on Jesus."[20]

The mistake made in both cases is the result of not
recognizing that for John it is the Word made flesh from
whom the argument starts. It is the Logos made flesh who
defines the Logos itself.

The point that is being made here can be illumined by
the way in which Cullmann explains the meaning of

[19] Kraemer, *op. cit.*, p. 438.
[20] Bultmann, *Jesus and the Word*, p. 278.

Jesus the Christ as the midpoint of history. The Christ line of redemptive history, he states, in its entirety is actually constructed from the midpoint. It is never possible to speak only of God without Christ.

> Even the time before the Creation is regarded entirely from the position of Christ; it is the time in which, in the counsel of God, Christ is already foreordained as Mediator before the foundation of the world. . . . He is then the Mediator in the Creation itself. . . . The Mediator of the Creation is the same one who as man, as "Son of Man," is to carry out on earth the decisive work of salvation. The election of the people of Israel takes place with reference to Christ and reaches its fulfillment in the work of the Incarnate One. But the present redemptive movement also is the working of Christ. Christ's role as Mediator continues in his Church, which indeed constitutes his earthly body. From it he exercises over heaven and earth the Lordship committed to him by God, though now it is invisible and can be apprehended only by faith. . . . Thus Christ is further the Mediator of the completion of the entire redemptive plan at the end. That is why he returns to the earth. . . . Upon the basis of his work the resurrection power of the Holy Spirit will transform all created things, including our mortal bodies; there will come into being a new heaven and a new earth in which sin and death no longer exist. Only then will Christ's role as Mediator be fulfilled. Only then will Christ "subject himself to him who subjected all things to him, in order that God may be all in all." . . . At that point only has the line which began with the Creation reached its end.[21]

This means that we cannot begin with the universal that became a particular, nor can we turn a particular into a universal, but that we affirm that here is the universal and the particular, the divine and the human, two natures but one person. As Barth quaintly puts it: "Only

[21] Cullmann, *op. cit.*, pp. 108–109.

in the phrase 'God and man' has the word 'and' its legitimate theological use. It declares the incomprehensible act by which the Word became flesh."[22]

It has seemed to me, reading what Bishop Robinson has written in *Honest to God,* that here was a third direction from which the centrality of the historical Jesus was impugned. The Bishop's argument rests on what the disciples and the contemporaries of Jesus saw.

> "And what God was, the Word was." In other words, if one looked at Jesus, one saw God—for "he who has seen me, has seen the Father." (HG, p. 71.)

> It is in Jesus, and Jesus alone, that there is nothing of self to be seen, but solely the ultimate, unconditional love of God. It is as he emptied himself utterly of himself that he became the carrier of "the name which is above every name," the revealer of the Father's glory— for that name and that glory is simply Love. (HG, p. 74.)

> In the man Christ Jesus stands revealed, exposed at the surface level of "flesh," the depth and ground of all our being as Love. (HG, p. 77.)

The fact, however, is that this way of seeing Jesus was for the disciples not the result of their life with Jesus of Nazareth but the result of the light thrown on that life by its culminating events in the crucifixion, the resurrection, and the ascension. In these events they saw the action of God, an action in accord with the central revelation of God in their scriptures, God as he rules and overrules the counsels of men, God as he submits himself and his purposes to defeat at man's hands only to turn defeat into final victory. Once they saw this, then they were able to see Jesus. It is not that they saw through him to the ground of his being, as Bishop Robinson says, but that they saw him and recognized who he was. He was the man Christ Jesus.

[22] Quoted by Donald Baillie in *God Was in Christ,* p. 83.

Bishop Robinson, in explanation of his position, quotes Tillich:

> The question of the final revelation [says Tillich] is the question of a medium of revelation which overcomes its own finite conditions by sacrificing them, and itself with them. He who is the bearer of the final revelation must surrender his finitude—not only his life but also his finite power and knowledge and perfection. In doing so, he affirms that he is the bearer of final revelation (the "Son of God" in classical terms). He became completely transparent to the mystery he reveals. But, in order to be able to surrender himself completely, he must possess himself completely. And only he can possess—and therefore surrender—himself completely who is united with the ground of his being and meaning without separation and disruption. In the picture of Jesus as the Christ we have the picture of a man who possesses these qualities, a man who, therefore, can be called the medium of final revelation.[23]

This whole method of speaking is at variance with the ambiguities concerning Jesus that his disciples and contemporaries felt. In Jesus of Nazareth, God was veiled. To speak of him as "completely transparent to the mystery he reveals" is to denigrate the actual happenings in the life of Jesus.

> But though the story [says Reinhold Niebuhr] is written from the standpoint of its special significance in the eyes of faith, it still embodies the perplexities of the disciples in accepting its true significance and the tortuous path by which Jesus moved against the obtuseness of his own disciples. It is not presented as a theophany, revealing the meaning of the eternal world to finite man; nor yet merely as the story of a "God-man" who overcame the breach between the eternal and the temporal or the divine and the temporal. On the contrary

[23] Tillich, *Systematic Theology*, Vol. I, p. 148.

it is a part of history though the claim is made that in
it history has found its true fulfilment.[24]

The passage in the Scriptures that Bishop Robinson
uses to set forward the point that he is trying to make is
taken from Paul's letter to the Philippians: "Who, though
he was in the form of God, did not count equality with
God a thing to be grasped, but emptied himself, taking
the form of a servant, being born in the likeness of men.
And being found in human form he humbled himself and
became obedient unto death, even death on a cross."
(Phil. 2:6–8.)

The thrust of this passage lies in the straight contrast
between *morphē theou* (the form of God) and *morphē
doulou* (the form of a slave). The right of Jesus as *morphē
theou* was the right to be worshiped and to be served.
("You shall worship the Lord your God and him only
shall you serve." Matt. 4:10; Deut. 6:13.) The temptation that Jesus faced was to grasp this right, but he set
it aside and took upon himself the task of bearing the
divine image as that image was in man ("So God created
man in his own image," Gen. 1:27). Man truly reflects
God as he serves him. To be *morphē doulou* is the true
consequence of bearing God's image. Whereas, in Adam,
man sought to grasp at equality with God, that decision
was reversed by the man Jesus. ("[He] came not to be
served but to serve," Mark 10:45.) Therein lay his vocation as Son of Man, as representative man. "He was born
in the likeness of men." This vocation Jesus carried out to
its final climax, accepting at the last, in full obedience,
the sentence of death, of death on a cross, a form of death
that carried with it the divine curse. (Gal. 3:13.) Therefore has God made him the one to be worshiped, and or-
dained that all shall worship him. In him and by him
man's history (from Adam) in sin has been reversed. In

[24] Niebuhr, *Faith and History,* pp. 163–164.

being man before God, He is now God before men. So
Paul urges on his fellow Christians, "Let your bearing
towards one another arise out of your life in Christ Jesus"
(Phil. 2:5, NEB).

The force of this passage, then, is not that Jesus emptied himself of his Godhead (which is the kenotic theory
of the incarnation) or that he emptied himself of himself
(which is what Bishop Robinson says), but that he lived
among men as man to God. Paul is speaking, not about
"Christ revealing God," which is what Bishop Robinson
takes as the theme of this passage, but about men living
in Christ Jesus because in him a new possibility for man
has arisen. This change of theme in the interpretation he
adopts is forced on the Bishop simply because he rejects
the possibility of the category of double action that Paul
uses—what Jesus did and what God did.

Actually, Bishop Robinson himself discovers the limita-
tions of his categories, for while in his polemic passages
he uses them and defends them, in many of his affirmations he frankly uses the normal language of the New
Testament.

Through him [Jesus] as through no one else, God spoke
and God acted: when one met him one was met—and
saved and judged—by God. And it was to this conviction that the Apostles bore their witness. In this man,
in his life, death and resurrection they had experienced
God at work. (HG, p. 71.)

Through the Resurrection God vindicated and set his
seal upon this man as the one through whom he spoke
and acted in final and decisive fashion. He vested himself[25] utterly and completely in the man Christ Jesus;

[25] One does not see how this way of speaking is different from
the two phrases that Bishop Robinson criticizes. (HG, p. 67.)
"Taking our nature upon him" and "Veiled in flesh the Godhead
see." The first phrase truly reflects Phil. 2:7 and the second is
an exact description of what happened in the earthly life of
Jesus.

in him all his fullness dwelt. What God was, the Word
was. (HG, pp. 72–73.)

It is only on the Cross that Jesus can be the bearer of
the final revelation and the embodiment of God's decisive acts. (HG, p. 74.)

It is by this mixing of two ways of speaking that Bishop
Robinson gives the impression that he is saying "the same
thing" in a different language when actually what he says
in this different language is again and again different
from the traditional confession of the faith. Nowhere does
this come out more clearly than in the way in which
Bishop Robinson explains the atonement wrought by
Christ. The plea he makes for a restatement of this doctrine is movingly made.

Most people would genuinely *like* to believe the Christ-
mas story, but wonder whether it *can* be true with the
world as it is after nearly two thousand years. But in
the case of the Atonement they ask with some im-
patience how anything done two thousand years ago on
the Cross *could* "affect me now." As a description of
some metaphysical *opus operatum* the "full, perfect and
sufficient sacrifice, oblation, and satisfaction for the sins
of the whole world" supposed to have been "made" on
Calvary requires, I believe, for most men today more
demythologizing even than the Resurrection. At no
point does the supranaturalist scheme appear less compelling. (HG, pp. 78–79.)

The whole schema of a supernatural Being coming
down from heaven to "save" mankind from sin, in the
way that a man might put his finger into a glass of
water to rescue a struggling insect, is frankly incredible
to man "come of age," who no longer believes in such a
deus ex machina. Yet Church people continue to explain the Atonement in some such terms as this,
picturing the interplay of two personified parties. (HG,
p. 78.)

How does the Bishop meet his own plea? He meets it by declaring that the atonement is recognized when we contemplate the new creation or the new man in Christ Jesus.

> It is nothing peculiarly religious—it is "neither circumcision nor uncircumcision." It is the life of "the man for others," the love whereby we are brought completely into one with the Ground of our being, manifesting itself in the unreconciled relationships of our existence. It was manifested supremely on the Cross, but it is met wherever the Christ is shown forth and recognized in "an entirely different mode of living-in-relationship from anything known in the world." For there, in however "secular" a form, is the atonement and the resurrection. (HG, p. 82.)

This is all very true, but if this be all the truth, then nothing really depends on what happened in the actual life of Jesus as it was actually lived or in his death and in his resurrection.

Any attempt simply to explain Jesus in terms of what men find in him does not do justice to the Biblical message. What happens in the New Testament is that Jesus is declared as God become man and that men find themselves led to the point of faith where they can so accept him. Such an acceptance makes sense of men's experience of Jesus. Men's experience of Jesus makes such an acceptance possible. But the acceptance itself is a gift of faith and is described as such, and this gift is grounded in the original miracle of the resurrection. This insistence not only on what men discover in Jesus but on what God did to and through Jesus is integral to the Biblical testimony. This cannot on any account be surrendered. If it cannot be stated within the categories chosen by Bishop Robinson, so much the worse for those categories. If, on the other hand, the Biblical categories are as offensive as John Wren-Lewis makes them out to be, then the witness

has to be made simply descriptively as the Gospels make
them.

The New Testament faith is that in Jesus of Nazareth
history did actually reach its midpoint and that not only
is history understood from this midpoint but is determined by it. The point of emphasizing what happened
two thousand years ago is to emphasize that it happened
within the stream of history and that therefore something
happened to human history itself.

> After Jesus lived and died in it, the world was never
> the same again. A new and spiritual energy entered into
> the process of human life. It is not exhausted: so far as
> one can see it never will be exhausted; and it may only
> now be entering upon a phase of plenary power.[26]

Part of the meaning of transcendence is that the history
of mankind transcends my personal history and that in
the history of mankind lies a divine transcendence to
which I am related both as subject and object.

A few years ago, I went to Perkins School of Theology
in Dallas, Texas, where I met with the students at a semi-
nar. No one had told me anything about the main theological influence in the college. For quite some time the
students could not understand what I was saying, nor
could I understand what they were saying. Then one
student said: "Let me put it simply so that you will understand. As far as we are concerned, the incarnation and
the resurrection are the same event." I said to him, "As
far as I am concerned, there is a difference of thirty-three
years between them." To this he replied, "But you are
talking about the Jesus of history." I asked him, "What
are you talking about?" and his answer was: "I am talking about Jesus and what he is to me. When I meet him,
when I am forgiven by him, that is the incarnation and

[26] John Middleton Murry, *Life of Jesus* (Jonathan Cape, Ltd.,
London, 1926), p. 70.

that is the resurrection." In other words, the gospel story provides us with an illustration of a fundamental human experience. It gives us certain categories in which that experience can be explained. But it in itself is not what the New Testament makes it out to be. My suspicion is that the Christ event of the New Testament, in terms of a deed of God in history, is discarded simply because it cannot be expressed in the already chosen categories of naturalism that understands transcendence only in the sense of self-transcendence. Self-transcendence is not an exhaustive understanding of transcendence.

What is the real implication of the Negro hymn that asks, "Were you there when they crucified my Lord?" Is not the implication that I was there and that you were there also? The men who crucified him were like us: we would have done the same. "I was there in Caiaphas who would save the nation by letting Jesus perish. I was there in Nicodemus who would not risk his position in the Sanhedrin for Jesus' sake. I was there in Peter who loved but was unprepared. I was there in Judas who followed but sought to bend Jesus to his own ends. I was there in Herod who did not care. I was there in Pilate who was afraid. I was there among the fickle crowd. I was one of the soldiers who simply did his duty."[27]

This is not just devotional imagination, for the situation is not that I have to go to Calvary to see myself there, but that the Crucified has come to me and is coming to me all the time. It is the fact of the resurrection that makes Jesus my contemporary and puts into my hands the power of life and death over him. But even more than this must be said.

> What crucified Jesus? The power of Rome was concerned with the maintenance of peace and order; and Jesus was a disturber of the peace. The Sadducees and

[27] D. T. Niles, *That They May Have Life* (Harper & Row, Publishers, Inc., 1951; Lutterworth Press, London, 1951), p. 55.

the house of the High Priest represented the culture of
the day. They were the guardians of local government
as well as trustees of the temple cult. Jesus seemed as
if he might bring the wrath of Rome upon them. He
also had attacked the cult. The Scribes were building
up a body of teaching to enable the common people to
observe the law. Jesus brushed aside the tradition of
the elders and pointed men to a God who is both living
and active in events. This was dangerous for ethical
living. The Pharisees were religious nationalists, the
flag of whose faith was the sabbath. Jesus tore that
flag down. The Herodians were the exponents of the
policy of *laissez faire;* while the Zealots sought to over-
throw the might of Rome, if need be, by force. The
Herodians found Jesus too intense for them, the Zealots
thought him too obtuse. Concern for peace and order,
enthusiasm for cult and culture, ardour for orthodoxy
in religion and nationalism in politics, desire for the
liberal way of life, passion for freedom from a foreign
yoke—these found Jesus dangerous. So was Jesus crucified by a combine of every form of human good brought
under the control of evil.[28]

The contemporaneousness of what happened two thousand years ago lies in its identity with the situation now.
It was the very stuff of the human situation that was
engaged in that event long ago.

Finally, what happened on Calvary was decisive because it happened to history as such. As Professor Stauffer puts it: "The Christ-event introduced a new situation
between God, the world and the adversary, and placed
the destiny of mankind on a new footing."[29] We are well
aware of the events and ideas that have changed the very
course of human history. In Jesus there was set up in
human history a whirlpool into which all events are being

28 *Ibid.,* pp. 21–22.
29 Ethelbert Stauffer, *New Testament Theology* (The Macmillan Company, 1955; SCM Press, Ltd., London, 1955), p. 159.

constantly sucked in. "Jesus," says Bishop Robinson, "is a window into God." It would be truer to say, using the New Testament word, that in him was the *kairos*. The straight meaning of the word *kairos* is "opening." To speak of the *kairos* is to speak of that moment of opportunity when time opens out into new possibilities. It is to speak of the nick of time, the moment when time has been nicked and its opportunity seized. It is also to speak of the decisive moment when a plan has come to its hour of fulfillment. How pointedly the writer of The Letter to the Hebrews underlines the once-for-all-ness of the historical moment of the Christ event! "If that were so, he would have had to suffer many times since the world was made. But as it is, he has appeared once and for all at the climax of history to abolish sin by the sacrifice of himself" (Heb. 9:26, NEB).

When we are speaking about Jesus of Nazareth, and all that he said and did, and all that happened to him, that which men did as well as that which God did, we are talking about this climax of history, this *kairos* that happened to the total story of man. And, because it was the *kairos*, it is part of the very reality of human history itself.

5

"God So Loved the World"

T HE GOSPEL ANNOUNCEMENT IS that the gift of God in Christ is eternal life. Eternal life is the life that God lives in the world. The Biblical testimony to "the living God" is a testimony to him at work in the world.

It is a remarkable fact that scarcely one of the Biblical writers is of the type of the pure mystic, rapt into another world and detached from temporal events. The prophets, it is true, had their visions of the world beyond this, but these visions bear direct reference to the needs and problems of their time. Their message does not unfold secrets of that other world, but interprets the events of this. When prophecy gives place to apocalypse, there is a growing tendency to dwell upon the unveiling of cosmic mysteries, but even here the main burden of apocalypse is always the course of events leading up to the expected climax. In the New Testament again, the apostle Paul, standing now in a world where mystical experience was highly valued, claims to have been caught up to Paradise and to have heard ineffable words; but he did not make a Gospel out of such raptures. With unimportant exceptions our writers are men immersed in the events of their time, and setting forth an interpretation of these events—an interpretation which itself passes into history. This is connected with the fact that the Hebrew mind, of which the Bible is the product, conceives God not as absolute

Being, but as the "living God," active in this world of
time and space, though not confined within it.[1]

When Peter confessed Jesus as the Christ, the Son of
the living God (Matt. 16:16), he was confessing not
only that Christ was the deed of God but also that Christ
was God himself at work. The Jewish expectation of the
Messiah was the expectation of God's direct intervention
in human history, whereby history would be reset in its
true direction and its culmination would be launched.
Peter was saying that this was precisely what had happened through Jesus.

The mission of God in Jesus Christ is an ongoing mission. There is the continuous and continuing ministry of
the risen Christ in the world. Christian discipleship is the
call to men and women to participate in this continuing
ministry. It is, in the words of Jesus, to drink of the cup
that he drank from and to be baptized with the baptism
that he was baptized with (Mark 10:38). When, therefore, the Evangelist says that God so loved the world, he
is saying that the news about God which the gospel an-
nounces is news about this world and for this world.

The calling of men is that they should not perish.
When a fruit has perished, it has to be thrown away.
When a tire has perished, it has to be discarded. Anything that has perished cannot be used anymore. But
the offer is that those who believe in Jesus Christ, that is,
those who have committed their lives to him and are prepared to follow him, will not perish. They will have eternal life. They will share in the life of God as God lives
his life in the world.

To Jesus has been given the name above every name
(Phil. 2:9), which is the name of God himself—Adonai:
so that the working of God in the world is unto the end
that all men shall come to live by his Lordship and all

[1] Dodd, *op. cit.*, pp. 30–31.

shall acknowledge that Jesus Christ rules as Lord. The controlling vision of the New Testament faith is the way in which the story of this world is ultimately brought within the story of God's redemptive action.

> In the three decisive stages of the Christ-line of salvation the general process is drawn into the redemptive process. It is so in Creation: everything is created through Christ. It is so in Christ's death and resurrection: everything is reconciled through him. It is so in the eschatological completion: everything is subjected to God, who is all in all.

> The general process of history takes its start from the same line as does the redemptive process, and it finally passes over into the same line. The present stage of redemptive history, since the resurrection of Christ, is already on the way back to that junction. Christ already rules over all things, but in a way visible only to faith. In proclaiming this fact, of which it knows by faith, the Church fulfills the task of carrying the development on to the goal where the now invisible Lordship of Christ will be visible to all.[2]

Here lies the reason why the Christian life is, in its essence, a life in the world for the world. It is not a religious exercise by which man in the natural world enters into a relationship with God in the supernatural world. A good example of this world connotation in the nature of the Christian life is the way in which, in the epistles, every great ethical section follows directly upon a discussion of the theological significance of the coming of God in Jesus Christ. In The Letter of Paul to the Romans, for instance, the twelfth chapter follows on eleven chapters of closely reasoned argument on the nature of the gospel. Paul says, "I appeal to you . . . to present your bodies as a living sacrifice. . . . Do not be conformed to this world." (Rom. 12:1-2.) There is a life that is natural to this world. The Christian life, on the other hand, arises out

[2] Cullmann, *op. cit.*, pp. 179, 184.

of the life of the Christian in Christ Jesus (Phil. 2:5, NEB).

The earliest term that was used to describe those who belonged to Jesus Christ was "men of the Way." (Acts 19:9, 23; 24:14.) By the use of this term it was clear that Christianity was not primarily conceived of as a religion; it was a particular way in which men lived and behaved in the world. The New Testament does not set this forward as a simple imitation of Christ. Jesus Christ is not just an example to be followed. Of course there is a true *imitatio Christi.* Peter speaks of Jesus as an example to be followed. "Christ also suffered for you, leaving you an example, that you should follow in his steps." (I Peter 2:21.) By the use of the vivid word *hupogrammos,* Peter is saying that in Jesus we have the outline sketch of the Christian life, the content of which has to be filled in by our Christian living. He is saying also that Jesus is the copy head in a writing exercise that men must learn to copy as the pattern of their writing.

But none know better than those who have sought to imitate Christ that such imitation inevitably leads to participation in the life he lived and still lives today.

The Master's call to his disciples to follow him was a call to follow him in a quite personal way, that is, to go with him wherever he goes, to be with him wherever he is, and to do with him whatever he does. The call to follow finds its meaning in the fact of the risen Christ, who is constantly going before us (Matt. 28:7) and who is ever with us all the way. "Unless a grain of wheat falls into the earth and dies, it remains alone; but if it dies, it bears much fruit." (John 12:24.) The Christian is the fruit of the dying of his Lord.

Christianity is not itself a New Testament word. The earliest equivalent of it is simply "the Way" or "the Road" and the first Christians spoke of themselves as following this road. Long before anybody called them Christians they spoke of themselves as the followers of

Jesus; and he himself had so spoken of them, his constant command being "Follow thou me." I rather think
that we have here a specifically Christian usage. Were
the disciples of any earlier teacher spoken of as his
followers—except in the colourless sense of those who
came after him in time? At all events, when our Lord
asked his first converts to follow him, he meant that
they should take the road with him—in a quite literal
sense. And I believe that when the Christians of the
next generation spoke of the Way and of themselves as
followers of Christ in the Way, they meant that they
were recapitulating the way he himself had travelled,
his journey up to Jerusalem and to the crucifixion. The
Way was the way of the Cross, in accordance with their
Lord's own word, "He who does not take up his cross
and follow me, is not worthy of me."[3]

In this understanding of the nature of Christianity lies
a true apprehension of its mission in the world. In the
New Testament the Christ event leads to a mission. As
the Fourth Evangelist has put it, the word of Jesus was,
"As the Father has sent me, even so I send you" (John
20:21), or as we read in The Acts of the Apostles, "You
shall be my witnesses [witnesses of what I have done and
what I shall continue to do] in Jerusalem and in all Judea
and Samaria and to the end of the earth" (Acts 1:8).
This mission is an exercise of the Lordship of Christ. It
arises from the fact that all authority everywhere is now
his. (Matt. 28:18.) Here again, veiled in the form of
an enterprise undertaken by men, is the presence of the
divine action and intervention.

The New Testament insists that the mission find its
embodiment and agent in a community—a community of
those who live by his love, who share his forgiveness, and
who, by their reconciled life, demonstrate his reconciling
power. They are those "upon whom the end of the ages
has come" (I Cor. 10:11). The end of history has hap-

[3] John Baillie, *The Sense of the Presence of God,* p. 137.

pened to them. This world and its concerns do not finally decide how they live or what they do. Their final stake is not here. (Phil. 3:20.) They proclaim the Lord's death till he comes. (I Cor. 11:26.)

No wonder the Christian mission is described by Paul as a pageant of Christ's triumph. (II Cor. 2:14.) Whatever else men see or may not see, they see men and women made captive by Jesus walking in his triumphal procession. Those who follow him have been captured by him and are evidences of his victory over their lives. They are also, says Paul, "for the praise of his glory" (Eph. 1:12). His glory is the splendor of his love poured out. This splendor is made the more splendid by their demonstration of his love as it works in them and through them. In suffering for others, they help to complete "the full tale of Christ's afflictions still to be endured" (Col. 1:24, NEB). This is eternal life. This is the victory that defeats the world.

> Indeed, they were and are right who find in God's will their only certainty of his grace. Having nothing themselves, they possess all things in Christ. Able only to ask forgiveness, they have received grace to render thanks. Mocked by the world, troubled in their consciences, they can nevertheless say: "I know whom I have believed." In the peace and joy to which the divine mercy daily brings them back, they fear "neither death nor life."[4]

Let us now pass from the question, What is the nature of Christianity? to the question, What is the nature of religion? In the contrast of the answer will come out the real import of all that we have said so far. This is a question to which I have given an extended answer in my book *Upon the Earth*.[5] I quote from it here.

[4] Maury, *op. cit.,* p. 68.
[5] Pp. 132–134. McGraw-Hill Book Company, Inc., 1962; Lutterworth Press, London, 1962. Copyright © 1962 D. T. Niles. Used by permission.

There are three aspects of the religious life which can
be distinguished. First of all, there is that aspect of religion which is concerned with a person's earthly life, his
material and physical needs, his joys and sorrows, his
ambitions and disappointments, his hopes and desires
for himself and his family and his friends. In this area
religion can mean either those practices of prayer and
religious discipline by which the divine aid is sought and
received, or those practices of renunciation and asceti-
cism by which the pressure of the earthly is reduced and
destroyed, or those practices which lie in the realm of
the magical and the occult by which the power of the
person over his surroundings and circumstances is in-
creased. With respect to all these there is real similarity
between the practices and prescriptions found in all religions, and all religions possess testimony about their ef-
ficacy. The Christian should not find this situation hard
to understand because he knows that God sends His rain
both on the just and the unjust, and makes his sun to
shine both on the good and the evil (Matt. 5:45). God's
care for all His children in their real need is a real care,
and it is exercised independently of man's so-called
religious practices. The criterion of truth as regards
religious practice, which is concerned with man's earthly
life and its need, is not the criterion of so-called success
but rather what that form of practice does to the human
spirit in its relation to God. Does it enable a person to
use the gifts of God for God's glory? Does it enable a
person to keep faith in God when the gift asked for is
not given? Does it teach a person to value God more
than His gifts? Does it train a person to grow in dis-
cernment about the gifts that he must ask?

Secondly, there is that aspect of religion which is at the
other end of the scale, where it is the very transitoriness
of life that has become oppressive, and where transcendence over this earthly life is the main concern. In
forms of religion where this is the climate, the main
drive is to overcome the manifoldness of life. The One
has become the many, and the religious urge is for the
many to know themselves as the One. When the self

transcends itself and overcomes all separation, then the religious goal has been attained. "Meditation" is the key word in this area of religion, and the transcendental mystic experience is the highest good. Once this experience is obtained, one may either withdraw from the life of the world into a life of contemplation, or live out one's earthly life displaying in one's work and relationships the graces that belong to the saints. In this form of religion too, all religions possess equally effective witnesses. When Paul speaks of being caught up to the third heaven and there witnessing what no words can describe (2 Cor. 12:2), he is speaking of an experience which is similar to that of transcendental mystics in all religions. No Christian should find it hard to believe that God who made man in His own image presents Himself to man's inner vision when He is sought after with persistence and diligence. Blessed are the pure in heart, for they shall see God (Matt. 5:8). "Ask," said Jesus. "Ask, and it will be given you. Seek, and you will find. Knock, and it will be opened to you. If you who are evil know how to give good gifts to your children, how much more will the heavenly Father give the Holy Spirit to those who ask Him?" (Lk. 11:9, 13).

There is a third aspect of religion in which the focus of attention is not this earthly life at all, neither its needs and problems nor its manifoldness. Neither the world nor the soul occupy the centre of the stage. Rather, the stage is occupied by God, and one feels intensely one's separation from Him. It is in this area that the problem of sin becomes acute. The religious life, therefore, becomes the quest for fellowship with God or for union with Him. This involves the removal of every barrier between man and God. Man must cease from his preoccupations with this life, and this is best done by practising habits of religion which will make God one's preoccupation. Man must overcome his divided interests between God and the world; this is achieved by practices of religious devotion which will fill the mind with thoughts of God and awaken in the soul an exclusive love of Him. Man must turn away from his sin and be forgiven; this is attained by casting oneself upon God's gracious mercy and by living the good life in the strength which He provides. And when every barrier is removed, the religious quest comes to its consummation in the enjoyment of the Divine. Here again in all religions there is similar evidence about man's wrestling with sin. There are indeed tremendous differences between the religions as to what constitutes sin: but all of them know the meaning of guilt and all of them carry evidence of men who found release from this sense of guilt each in his own way and according to his own faith.

All these three aspects of religion have religious validity and there is witness for this from men in every religion. At their base, the institutional forms of all religions are directed towards the same concerns; and the mystics among them, in the last analysis, speak the same language.

We thus see that the religious life arises from three aspects of life all of which are common to all men—man's creatureliness, the transitoriness of human life, and man's sinfulness. The counterpoint in God of each of these aspects is that God is creator of all men, that all men are created in his image, and that toward all men God is love. So that, speaking religiously, Christianity is just one religion among many.

But if all that we have already said about the essential nature of the Christian faith is true, then to speak of Christianity as a religion is like saying that man is an animal except that he has some peculiar features. The point is that what is peculiar about man is so determinative of him that this peculiarity makes it impossible to speak of him as an animal with any real relevance.

How, then, is the relation between Christianity and the religions, and between Christianity and itself as a religion, best understood? A true answer to this question can serve to underline the real nature of the Christian faith.

A diagrammatic presentation can help to make the answer clear: If one draws a circle to represent the totality of all things, then one would say that the center of this circle is Jesus Christ.[6] There is nothing outside his rule, in him all things cohere, all things are through him and for him. (Col. 1:16–17.) But in the long story of man, men have refused to acknowledge his Lordship or to be obedient to it. They have created other centers around which to build their lives.

The various religions, including modern religions like humanism, scientism, Marxism, can be represented as circles, within the large circle, drawn around their various centers. These centers are by their nature in opposition to the true center, but they find their power by being within the circle which the true center describes. To use a sentence of Walter Freytag, "Men use God against God." The Christian religion, however, must be designated, not as a circle, but as an ellipse. While Jesus Christ remains a center, there is set up another center. The result is that these two foci describe an ellipse. Sinful men never find it possible to abide by the circle. The second focus is the result sometimes of absolutizing some partial truth, sometimes of insisting on some particular historical form, sometimes of introducing into the Christian faith a disguised dependence on "good works," sometimes of finding for prejudice and sin a false rationalization, and so on. Here lies the wretchedness of the church. The centers around which the religions are organized constitute a rejection of Jesus Christ. The second focus in the Christian religion constitutes an attitude of rebellion against him.

The direction in which the argument of this chapter

[6] The gospel is the revelation or manifestation—not of another religion but—"of Him who is the Living Centre of the Universe, the assertion that all men are related to Him; the destruction of every wall of partition between Man and Man; the admission of all who desire it into fellowship with the Father of the whole family in Heaven and Earth." (F. D. Maurice, quoted by A. R. Vidler, ed., in *Soundings*, p. 242.)

is set is toward a consideration of Dietrich Bonhoeffer's plea for a religionless Christianity. But, before we listen to that plea and what it implies, it is essential to clarify still further the discussion on the nature of the Christian faith and the nature of the religions, including Christianity.

> God's revelation is the annulment of religion [says Karl Barth]. The event of revelation does not have two aspects: God the agent and man the recipient. Both the act of revelation and its reception are God's. Revelation is God's sovereign dealing with man, or it is not revelation. It is an event that happens to man, although it must be added that it takes shape in human religious experience and action. In this respect revelation has a human face. This human psychological, historical face and structure is what we call the Christian religion. As such, it stands alongside other religious "faces," and is not unique, but has its peculiar character. This means that the true theological judgment on religion as religion is that it is unbelief. There is no true religion, just as there is no good man.[7]

Here we have a thoroughgoing statement of the position we have outlined of religions as being built around false centers; but as Kraemer points out, this statement is an oversimplification.

> It has the unintentional effect of blocking the entrance into the reality of the living religions as embodiments of the drama between God and man. It keeps religion and the religions in their place, but it establishes no contact and no real encounters.[8]

We may not forget the truth that the false centers are always under the constant pressure of the true center,

[7] Barth, *Church Dogmatics*, Vol. I, Part 2 (*passim*).
[8] Kraemer, *op. cit.*, p. 193.

and that man in his separation from God is still haunted by Him, seeking for Him in the midst of his very rebellion.

No wonder that when Christ enters the religious consciousness of man, he enters it as a revolutionary. As P. Chenchiah puts it, both trenchantly and concretely:

> The supreme longing of the Hindu after escape from samsara is not satisfied by Christ. The gift of Rebirth as offered by Christ does not appeal to the Hindu. On the contrary, Jesus kindles new hopes not felt before and kills some of the deepest and most persistent longings of man.[9]

If this is so, we must be prepared to say two things: that, in the first place, there is within the world of religions such a true seeking and finding of God as to make meaningful, to those who have this experience, Christ's call to give up the religious posture altogether; and, in the second place, that the exclusive religious quality of the other religions can truly reveal to Christianity as a religion how widely it has departed from its original impulse.

> Under many names, names which are not that of God, in ways only known to God, the interior act of a soul's thought can be directed towards a reality which in fact truly may be God.[10]

> I was ready to be sought by those who did not ask for me; I was ready to be found by those who did not seek me. (Isa. 65:1; cf. Rom. 10:20.)

> The service which we ought to expect from other Faiths, in their encounter with us, is that they should shake up our Christianity and turn it into an authentic bearer of the Divine message. It is from other Faiths

[9] Quoted in Kraemer, *op. cit.*, pp. 215 f.
[10] Jacques Maritain, *True Humanism* (Charles Scribner's Sons, 1938; Geoffrey Bles, Ltd., Publishers, London, 1938), p. 56.

that we learn how great is the gulf between Christianity and the Gospel.[11]

Let us now turn to look at the implications of the plea that Dietrich Bonhoeffer makes for a religionless Christianity. First of all, he is asking that the Christian life should be conceived not in terms of God's usefulness to man, however religious man's needs may be, but in terms of man's participation in the life of God as He lives it in the world in weakness and in suffering. For the continuing ministry of Christ in the world is still the ministry of the cross.

> Men go to God when he is sore bested: find him poor and scorned, without shelter and bread, whelmed under weight of the wicked, the weak, the dead. Christians stand by God in his hour of grieving.[12]

> The Old Testament speaks of historical redemption, i.e., redemption on this side of death, whereas the myths of salvation are concerned to offer men deliverance from death. . . . The salvation myths deny history in the interests of an eternity after death. . . . The difference between the Christian hope of resurrection and a mythological hope is that the Christian hope sends a man back to his life on earth in a wholly new way which is even more sharply defined than it is in the Old Testament. The Christian, unlike the devotees of the salvation myths, does not need a last refuge in the eternal from earthly tasks and difficulties. But like Christ himself he must drink the earthly cup to the lees, and only in his doing that is the crucified and risen Lord with him, and he crucified and risen with Christ. This world must not be prematurely written off. In this

---

[11] Heinrich Frick, *The Gospel, Christianity, and Other Faiths,* tr. by James Haire (Basil Blackwell & Mott, Ltd., Oxford, 1938), p. 63.

[12] Dietrich Bonhoeffer, *The Cost of Discipleship,* tr. by R. H. Fuller (The Macmillan Company, 1949; SCM Press, Ltd., London, 1948), p. 20.

the Old and New Testaments are at one. Myths of salvation arise from human experiences of the boundary situation. Christ takes hold of man in the centre of his life.[13]

Secondly, Bonhoeffer is asking that the world and life in the world be understood not in religious terms but in secular terms. He is asking, not that a space should be cleared for religion in the life of the world, but that the life of the world itself should be taken seriously with the seriousness of God.

We should find God in what we do know, not in what we don't; not in outstanding problems, but in those we have already solved. This is true not only for the relation between Christianity and science, but also for wider human problems such as guilt, suffering and death. It is possible nowadays to find answers to these problems which leave God right out of the picture. It just isn't true to say that Christianity alone has the answers. In fact the Christian answers are no more conclusive or compelling than any of the others. Once more, God cannot be used as a stop-gap. We must not wait until we are at the end of our tether: he must be found at the centre of life: in life, and not only in death; in health and vigour, and not only in suffering; in activity, and not only in sin. The ground for this lies in the revelation of God in Christ. Christ is the centre of life, and in no sense did he come to answer our unsolved problems. From the centre of life certain questions are seen to be wholly irrelevant, and so are the answers commonly given to them. In Christ there are no Christian problems.[14]

And thirdly, Bonhoeffer is asking that the message of the gospel be so presented that obedience to it is seen not to rest on the religious premise or on any religious tradi-

[13] Bonhoeffer, *Letters and Papers from Prison,* pp. 153–154.
[14] *Ibid.,* pp. 142–143.

tion. By the religious premise he means God as the answer to man's questionings on the boundaries of his
knowledge, or God as the solace of conscience and of the
anxieties of man's interior life. The example he gives of
what he means by religious tradition is that of circumcision, referring to the demand made on the early church
that the Christian life must fit into the religious life as it
was known and lived in that day.[15]

Since at this point we shall pass to a discussion of the
way in which Bishop Robinson relates the teachings of
Tillich, Bultmann, and Bonhoeffer, we shall give here a
long quotation from Bonhoeffer himself where this relation is treated.

> Tillich set out to interpret the evolution of the world
> itself—against its will—in a religious sense, to give it
> its whole shape through religion. That was very coura-
> geous of him, but the world unseated him and went on
> by itself: he too sought to understand the world better
> than it understood itself, but it felt entirely misunder-
> stood, and rejected the imputation. Barth was the first
> to realise the mistake that all these efforts were making
> in having as their objective the clearing of a space for
> religion in the world or against the world. He called the
> God of Jesus Christ into the lists against religion,
> "pneuma against sarx." That was and is his greatest
> service. Bultmann would seem to have felt Barth's limi-
> tations in some way, but he misconstrues them in the
> light of liberal theology, and hence goes off into the
> typical liberal reduction process (the "mythological"
> elements of Christianity are dropped, and Christianity
> is reduced to its "essence"). I am of the view that the
> full content, including the mythological concepts, must
> be maintained. The New Testament is not a myth-

[15] For an incisive discussion of the concepts of "religionless
Christianity" and "holy worldliness," see the book by Daniel
Jenkins entitled *Beyond Religion* (The Westminster Press, 1962;
SCM Press, Ltd., London, 1962).

ological garbing of the universal truth; this mythology (resurrection and so on) is the thing itself—but the concepts must be interpreted in such a way as not to make religion a pre-condition of faith.[16]

One of the biggest confusions in Bishop Robinson's argument is the result of assuming that Bonhoeffer's protest against religion is in the same direction as Tillich's protest against supranaturalism. Let us listen to Tillich again:

> Our period has decided for a secular world. That was a great and much-needed decision. . . . It gave consecration and holiness to our daily life and work. Yet it excluded those deep things for which religion stands: the feeling for the inexhaustible mystery of life, the grip of an ultimate meaning of existence, and the invincible power of an unconditional devotion. These things *cannot* be excluded.[17]

Bonhoeffer's position is the exact opposite of this. His protest is against religion "on the borders of life" which in Tillich are "the depths of being." He asks, on the other hand, for a concern with God at the center. "God is the beyond" in the midst of our life. Bishop Robinson seeks to equate this position of Bonhoeffer with Tillich's concept of self-transcendence. Tillich is talking about the transcendent quality of the self, Bonhoeffer is talking about the beyond as it has come and as it dwells and as it manifests itself in our midst. The stress is not on the beyondness of what is ours but on the importance of recognizing that it is in our midst. "The kingdom of God has come near to you. . . . [It] has come upon you. . . . [It] is in the midst of you." (Luke 10:9; 11:20; 17:21.)

> What is above the world is, in the Gospel, intended to exist for this world—I mean that not in the anthropo-

16 Bonhoeffer, *Letters and Papers from Prison,* pp. 147–149.
17 Tillich, *The Shaking of the Foundations,* p. 181.

centric sense of liberal, pietistic, ethical theology, but in the Bible sense of the creation and of the incarnation, crucifixion, and resurrection of Jesus Christ.[18]

The confusion created by attempting an amalgam of Tillich and Bonhoeffer is made worse when Bishop Robinson assumes that Bultmann's protest against myth has the same consequence as Bonhoeffer's protest against religion. Bonhoeffer himself says that the mythological conceptions such as the miracles, the ascension, and the like, while they are problematic, are not in principle separable from the conceptions of God, faith, and so on. He says the religious conceptions themselves are problematic.

> You cannot, as Bultmann imagines, separate God and miracles, but you do have to be able to interpret and proclaim both of them in a "non-religious" sense.[19]

The point is that as long as the gospel is allowed to be treated as a religious tradition, demythologizing its concepts takes us nowhere.

Bonhoeffer himself has left us the outline of a book, which he never lived to write, where he sets out the direction in which he thought the answers to his own questions lay.

1. He saw that man's predicament in the future was going to be a world "come of age" wherein man had organized for himself both welfare and security. But this organization of the world was itself going to be man's real problem. With the decay of religion as such would arise the need for a spiritual vitality that would enable men to live in the world that they had organized.

2. The true test and dimension of this spiritual vitality would be the willingness to take risks in the service of humanity. It is to this risk that the church is summoned.

[18] Bonhoeffer, *Letters and Papers from Prison,* p. 126.
[19] *Ibid.,* p. 125.

3. The source of this spiritual vitality is the encounter with Jesus Christ. Jesus is the one whose only concern is for others. This concern of Jesus for others is the experience of transcendence that we have when we meet him.

4. The omnipotence, omniscience and ubiquity of Jesus are grounded solely in his freedom from self, maintained to the point of death.

5. Faith is participation in this Being of Jesus (incarnation, cross, and resurrection). This participation issues in a new life for others. This is participation in the Being of God.

6. To think of our relation to God as a religious relationship to a supreme being, absolute in power and goodness, is a spurious conception of transcendence.

7. The transcendence consists not in tasks beyond our scope and power, but in the nearest Thou to hand: God in human form and man existing for others, and hence the Crucified.

8. What we do really believe is what we believe in such a way as to stake our whole lives upon it.[20]

The "Being" of Jesus and the "Being" of God are the key terms in this statement: also the concept that one encounters the transcendent in encountering Jesus. It seems to me impossible to evade the conclusion that what Bonhoeffer is talking about is the Being of Jesus in the world, the Being of God in the world. Jesus is in the world, and the way he is in the world is as the Man for others. It is this fact which gives to him omnipotence, omniscience and ubiquity. We meet him in our dealing with others because of his concern for them, and in that meeting we find ourselves faced by omnipotence (unyielding demand), omniscience (refusal to accept any reservation or subterfuge), and ubiquity (for no one is outside his concern). The protest against religion is protest against man's

[20] *Ibid.,* p. 179. (Compare the paraphrase and arrangement under eight headings that are given above with the original.)

attempts to deal with God as God and not as God for and with men.

Here lies the final implication of the title of this chapter: "God so loved the world." The world is not simply a geographical term; it denotes life in the total range and complexity of its relationships. It is this world which God loved. And because he loved it, he made for all men one trysting place, that there they might find him as well as one another. Toynbee quotes the Roman senator Symmachus, exclaiming, in his controversy with Saint Ambrose, on behalf of the religions of ancient Rome:

> "It is impossible that so great a mystery should be approached by one road only." The mystery of which he is speaking [Toynbee comments] is the mystery of the Universe, the mystery of Man's encounter with God, the mystery of God's relation to good and evil. Christianity has never answered Symmachus. To suppress a rival religion is not an answer. The question raised by Symmachus is still alive in the World today. I think we shall have to face it in our time.[21]

There is no way of facing this question, and no way of facing the answer to it which Christianity gives, as long as one keeps on talking about religion, that is, man's approach to God's mystery. The universalism for which Toynbee pleads atomizes the human community. Each can go his own way to God, and therefore one can find God without finding his brother. But because God loved the world, he has provided for the world one center, one act of acknowledgment. He has involved men in a common finding rather than in a common search. The unity of religions, Radhakrishnan contends, lies in a common quest.[22] But the concern of God as the Bible speaks of

[21] Toynbee, *op. cit.,* p. 112.

[22] Sarvepalli Radhakrishnan, *The Hindu View of Life* (The Macmillan Company, 1926; George Allen & Unwin, London, 1926), p. 58.

him is not the unity of religions but the unity of mankind.

This unity has been wrought for men. In Jesus, God has set men free from their enslavement to the forces inherent in nature and history, forces whose propitiation was man's nightmare. In Jesus, God has set men free from the limitation of their own resources of knowledge and vision. In Jesus, God has set men free from the temptation to turn God himself into a means for man. In Jesus, God has delivered men also from that false freedom in which men would rather live with universals that they can manipulate than with a particular to which they are bound.

To underline each of the four points made here, let me give a quotation from Dr. Visser 't Hooft's latest book, *No Other Name.*

The "life-force" of D. H. Lawrence, the "archetypes" of Jung, the "spirits" of spiritualism, the *"karma"* of theosophy and other syncretisms are all impersonal powers which confront man with an "it" instead of confronting him with the "Thou" who is the living God revealed in Jesus Christ.

Now a God who speaks in an infinite variety of ways but never decisively really throws man back upon himself, for it is then up to man to determine how and where he can reach ultimate truth. Thus the syncretisms conceive of religion as a system of insights and concepts rather than as a dialogical relation between a personal God and his creature.

There is a famous statement of Gibbon: "The various *modi* of worship which prevailed in the Roman world were all considered by the people equally true, by the philosophers equally false, and by the magistrates equally useful." . . . The magistrates seem to have changed least of all. Has it not been reported that Mr. Eisenhower has echoed the words of Gibbon by saying:

"Our government makes no sense unless it is founded in a deeply felt religious faith—and I don't care what it is"?

Yes, if Christianity can dispense with the deeds of God, the events of the history of salvation, then it is possible to arrive at a synthesis on the basis of a timeless mysticism. And then it is conceivable that, as Professor Hocking thinks, it will become part of a world-religion which may or may not use the name of Christ, but which will represent an extension of the concept of the Christ to include that unbound Spirit who stands and has stood at the door of every man. But in that case we are no longer concerned with the real Jesus whom we find in the New Testament. We are only left with a Christ-concept vaguely related to the historical record.[23]

To meet God in Christ in the world—that is the cutting edge of the Christian invitation: to acknowledge what happens when thus we meet is the beginning of the Christian life. What happens? We meet him and because in that meeting he is at our mercy and at our disposal we reject him. He dies at our hands. When, however, we acknowledge what we have done we see that his death is for us. If we did not kill him, he did not die for us. But he continues to give himself to us—he is the risen Lord —so that, in receiving him and in being received by him, we find for our lives a new beginning. We become participants in the New Being in Christ.

But this encounter with Jesus Christ cannot be for us a purely contemporaneous event. We meet him—the same Jesus—embedded in history; we meet him in the fellowship of the community whom he indwells, and in his prevailing concern for all men who are, for us, those for whom he died. Thus do we find ourselves caught up

[23] W. A. Visser 't Hooft, *No Other Name* (The Westminster Press, 1964; SCM Press, Ltd., London, 1963), pp. 91, 48, 49, 34.

in the love of God—his love for his world and its count-
less generations, and his love for us, each in his own
particularity. Thus also do we find ourselves caught up in
loving him.

But do we really love him?

> You want [says the Abbé Henri de Tourville] to com-
> pete with His affection before you have understood it;
> that is your mistake. . . . Come then! Show a little
> more deference to our Lord and allow Him to go first.
> Let Him love you a great deal before you have suc-
> ceeded in loving Him even a little as you would wish to
> love Him. That is all I ask of you, and all that our Lord
> asks of you.[24]

[24] Abbé Henri de Tourville, *Letters of Direction* (Thomas Y.
Crowell Company, 1939; Adam & Charles Black, Ltd., London,
1939), pp. 78 ff.

6

"For You Have Died"

THE CHRISTIAN COMMUNITY is evidence of something that has happened. It bears the marks of "a fallout" of an atomic explosion. Jesus of Nazareth lived and died and rose from the dead. The consequence of this event for others is that to them is opened the possibility to end their natural lives by bringing them under his judgment, so that in him and through him they might live the life that is his. "For you have died, and your life is hid with Christ in God." (Col. 3:3.)

When Jesus said, "I am . . . the life" (John 11:25; 14:6), he was asserting that he was the life we had to live. It is not that we have to live as he lived but that we have to live him. To use Bonhoeffer's phrase, the principle of the Christian life is "how Christ takes form among us here and now."[1] Two incidents from the Gospels illustrate the major implications of this truth. When a man addressed Jesus as "Good Teacher," Jesus said to him, "No one is good but God alone" (Mark 10:17–18). Jesus insists on standing on that side of the line where all men stand. He is man. But, having established that position, he tells his questioner, "Sell what

---

[1] Dietrich Bonhoeffer, *Ethics,* ed. by E. Bethge (The Macmillan Company, 1955; SCM Press, Ltd., London, 1955), pp. 18–19. Reprinted with permission of The Macmillan Company. Copyright 1955 by The Macmillan Company.

you have, . . . and come, follow me." To inherit eternal
life is to remain man with men and with the Son of Man,
but it is to remain with them as the follower of this Son
of Man, Jesus. God alone has the right to make the demand "Follow me," but, in that God makes it by Jesus,
the demand is made from man as such and not from
religious man. The man who came to Jesus was religious.
He had kept the law. What he lacked was "nonreligion":
for what does it profit a man if he gains his own soul and
loses the whole world? (Cf. Matt. 16:26.) You lack one
thing; go, sell what you have, and give to the poor, and
you will have treasure in heaven.

In the parable of the sheep and the goats, the identifi-
cation of Jesus with man is given explicit reference. "I
was hungry . . . I was thirsty . . . I was a stranger . . . I
was in prison." (Matt. 25:31–46.) But these men with
whom Jesus is identified are all marginal men. They are
those on the margin of society, unable to protect themselves, at other men's mercy, in need of the kindness of
others. Both the Old and New Testaments insist that God
keeps a strict account of other men's obligations to marginal people—the widow, the fatherless, the orphans, the
poor, the stranger, the prisoner, the slave. The peculiarity
of the presence of Jesus in the world lies precisely here;
it is that he lives among us as one whom we may despise,
ill-treat, and reject. "Jesus . . . became poor." (II Cor.
8:9.)

To put it sharply, the Christian ethic is defined by the
presence of Christ with men, among men, and as men: so
that the two commandments "Love God" and "Love your
neighbor" cohere in one person. More than that, they
inhere in each situation, so that "Give to the poor" and
"Follow me" become parts of a single obedience.

There are two sayings of Jesus referring to the relationship between parents and children, the closest human
relationship, that warns us against a false understanding

of the mutual implications of the two commandments. There were those who made the love of God an obligation whose content was independent of human relationships. They said that even one's duties to one's parents could be set aside as corban—that is, offered to God. (Mark 7:11.) Jesus characterized this as a rejection of God's commandment. There were others who would make the love of man the way to love God. How irrevocably this position is shattered by the words of Jesus: "If any one comes to me and does not hate his own father and mother and wife and children and brothers and sisters, yes, and even his own life, he cannot be my disciple."[2]

Bishop Robinson pleads in his book for a situational ethic in which right and wrong are not decided by universals. He rightly claims that Christian ethics is non-prescriptive and that "the right thing to do" does not arrive from "out there."

> What the supranaturalist ethic does [he says] is to subordinate the actual individual relationship to some universal, whether metaphysical or moral, external to it. The decision is not reached, the judgement is not made, on the empirical realities of the particular concrete relationship between the persons concerned. Man is made for the sabbath, and not the sabbath for man. Be the individual circumstances what they will, the moral law is the same—for all men and for all times. It is imposed on the relationship from without, from above: the function of casuistry is to "apply" it *to* the case in question.

> Such an ethic is "heteronomous," in the sense that it derives its norm from "out there"; and this is, of

[2] Luke 14:26. How hopelessly one-track the situation becomes if, as Bishop Robinson suggests (HG, p. 60), the words of Jeremiah are taken to be a sufficient and unqualified definition of what it means to know God. "Did not your father eat and drink and do justice and righteousness? Then it was well with him. He judged the cause of the poor and needy; then it was well. *Is not this to know me?* says the Lord." (Jer. 22:15–16.)

course, its strength. It stands for "absolute," "objective" moral values and presents a dyke against the floods of relativism and subjectivism. And yet this heteronomy is also its profound weakness. Except to the man who believes in "the God out there" it has no compelling sanction or self-authenticating foundation. It cannot answer the question *"Why* is this wrong?" in terms of the intrinsic realities of the situation itself. (HG, pp. 112–113.)

But, in defining the intrinsic realities of the situation, Bishop Robinson takes his stand on the position that the Christian ethic is for all men and is based upon the nature of man.

The Christian ethic is not relevant merely for the Christian, still less merely for the religious. The claim of the Christ may come to others, as indeed it often comes to the Christian, incognito: but since it is the claim of home, of the personal ground of our very being, it does not come as anything foreign. (HG, p. 115.)

This claim of the Christ, says Bishop Robinson, is the claim of love.

This is what it means for the Christian to "have the mind of Christ," to let his actions be governed, as Jesus enjoined, simply and solely by the love with which "I have loved you." . . . Life in Christ Jesus, in the new being, in the Spirit, means having no absolutes but his love, being totally uncommitted in every other respect but totally committed in this. (HG, p. 114.)

In Tillich's words:

Love alone can transform itself according to the concrete demands of every individual and social situation without losing its eternity and dignity and unconditional validity.[3]

3 Paul Tillich, *The Protestant Era,* p. 173.

The intrinsic problem in this thesis lies at the point where the transcendent quality of the Christian life is defined in terms of the nature of man and what Bishop Robinson has called his self-transcendence. In actual fact, if, as Bishop Robinson himself says, the governing principle is the love with which Christ has loved us, then his love does not arise from our nature at all.

What henceforth determines our actions is not a principle of love but the fact that we have been loved and are loved all the time. The determining factor in the situation is that Christ has laid hold upon me. I have died because of him, and now in him I find myself living him who is the life. To put it differently, the compulsion to love is not a Christian compulsion except as it arises from and is controlled by the incursion of grace. In The First Letter of John, the proof that we have passed from death to life is made to rest on the discovery that we now find it possible to love the brethren. (I John 3:14.)

In a previous chapter we have maintained the position that God's grace and its operation are the reality that the concept of transcendence is designed to set out.

> The transcendence of God [Bultmann has said] and His grace are one and the same thing. The Cross of Christ, which is God's judgment over the world and the means by which he makes the wisdom of this world foolishness, is the revelation of his grace. The man who accepts the Cross as God's judgment upon himself is delivered from the world.[4]

Paul states this truth in the simplest and most direct language in his second letter to the Corinthians. "Examine yourselves," he says, "to see whether you are holding to your faith. Test yourselves. Do you not realize that Jesus Christ is in you?—unless indeed you fail to meet the test!" (II Cor. 13:5.)

[4] Rudolf Bultmann, *Primitive Christianity* (Thames & Hudson, Ltd., London, 1956), pp. 230–231.

The compulsion to love springs out of this incursion of grace precisely because this grace is grace for all men. In the first place, it does not come to me apart from its involvement in other people. To be found by Jesus is to find that he whom I thought was a stranger is actually my brother. It is to find also that I am implicated in the love of Jesus for him. This discovery has for the Christian a center and a circumference. The center is the Christian fellowship. He loved us, and because he loved us, together we must love one another (I John 4:19–20).

> The Christian Way, then, is the way followed within the *koinōnia* of *agapē,* and is a form of togetherness specific to Christianity in spite of all foreshadowings of it that may elsewhere be found. In all probability it was St. Paul who introduced the term *agapē* into Christian discourse, and he used it to differentiate the characteristic life of the Christian *koinōnia* from that which he had formerly known within the synagogue. The togetherness is essentially that of a triangular relationship, the three angles of which were oneself, one's fellow Christians, and God as known in Christ; and the relationship is such that from any one angle a second angle can be effectively reached only by way of the third.[5]

The formula of Cyprian: *"Extra ecclesiam nulla salus"* is translated by John Baillie—"the man who keeps to himself cannot be made whole."

But precisely because this is the center of the Christian ethic, there radiates from this center a widening circumference that includes all men. Bonhoeffer makes our obligation to our fellowmen rest on the concern that Jesus has for them. It is his concern for them and his busyness with them that define their situation.

> Christ teaches no abstract ethics such as must at all costs be put into practice. Christ was not essentially a

[5] John Baillie, *The Sense of the Presence of God,* pp. 138–139.

teacher and legislator, but a man, a real man like ourselves. And it is not therefore His will that we should in
our time be the adherents, exponents and advocates of
a definite doctrine, but that we should be men, real
men before God. Christ did not, like a moralist, love a
theory of good, but He loved the real man. He was not,
like a philosopher, interested in the "universally valid,"
but rather in that which is of help to the real and concrete human being. What worried Him was not, like
Kant, whether "the maxim of an action can become a
principle of general legislation," but whether my action
is at this moment helping my neighbour to become a
man before God.[6]

To speak of the situation, therefore, is to speak about
Jesus Christ. It is to speak about me in Christ, it is to
speak about my fellowmen in Christ, and it is to speak
about Christ in the fellowship. Archbishop Ramsey says
of the chapter on "The New Morality" in Bishop Robinson's book that what we find in it is a "deductive theory
from the concept of love."[7] How right the Archbishop is
can be seen from the fact that Bishop Robinson sees in
the paganism of D. H. Lawrence "a way through here to
the transcendent in a world without religion." (HG, p.
121.) Simply because D. H. Lawrence uses words that
are emotionally the same as words used by Bonhoeffer,
the Bishop concludes that this emotion is transferable to
God the Father of our Lord Jesus Christ. The crux of the
matter is that we must go beyond (to use the Bishop's
terms) not only heteronomy and autonomy, but also
theonomy. Self-transcendence still leaves us at the mercy
of the gods, only the transcendence of God's grace in
Christ can set our feet on rock. We are, then, no more
left with a principle of love, whether regulative or constitutive; we are controlled by one who loves and whose
active love is the determinant in all relationships.

[6] Bonhoeffer, *Ethics*, p. 22.
[7] Ramsey, *op. cit.*, p. 14.

Henceforward one can speak neither of God nor of the world without speaking of Jesus Christ. All concepts of reality which do not take account of Him are abstractions. When good has become reality in Jesus Christ, there is no more force in any discussion of good which plays off what should be against what is and what is against what should be. Jesus Christ cannot be identified with an ideal or standard or with things as they are. The hostility of the ideal towards things as they are, the fanatical putting into effect of an idea in the face of a resisting actuality, may be as remote from good as is the sacrifice of what should be to what is expedient. Both what should be and what is expedient acquire in Christ an entirely new meaning. The irreconcilable conflict between what is and what should be is reconciled in Christ, that is to say, in the ultimate reality. Participation in this reality is the true sense and purpose of the enquiry concerning good.[8]

If our argument up to this point has some validity, then it is clear that it is misleading to speak of the Christian ethic as an ethic for all men. It is certainly for all men, but in that sense it is an offer and a challenge to all men to belong to Jesus Christ and to acknowledge his Lordship.

The claim of the Christ [says Bishop Robinson] may come to others, as indeed it often comes to the Christian, incognito: but since it is the claim of home, of the personal ground of our very being, it does not come as anything foreign. It is neither heteronomous nor autonomous but theonomous. (HG, p. 115.)

But precisely in the possibility that men may and do accept and obey the Christ incognito lies the imperative to proclaim the Christ, that men may accept him openly and own his Lordship. "What therefore you worship as unknown, this I proclaim to you." (Acts 17:23.) The obligations of love as felt in the depths of our being are delivered from the relativisms imposed by human sin,

[8] Bonhoeffer, *Ethics*, p. 61.

which is part of our nature, only as this love compulsion is itself cleansed by Jesus Christ and always held under the judgment of his life as it was actually lived.

> Ecce homo!—Behold the man! In Him the world was reconciled with God. It is not by its overthrowing but by its reconciliation that the world is subdued. It is not by ideals and programmes or by conscience, duty, responsibility and virtue that reality can be confronted and overcome, but simply and solely by the perfect love of God. Here again it is not by a general idea of love that this is achieved, but by the really lived love of God in Jesus Christ.[9]

The argument must now be pressed forward to the other emphasis that Bishop Robinson makes: "It is love which is the constitutive principle—and law, at most, is only the regulative one, if it is even that." (HG, p. 116.)

> *What* "love's casuistry" requires makes, of course, the most searching demands both upon the depth and integrity of one's concern for the other—whether it is really the utterly unselfregarding *agape* of Christ—and upon the calculation of what is truly the most loving thing in this situation for every person involved. Such an ethic cannot but rely, in deep humility, upon guiding rules, upon the cumulative experience of one's own and other people's obedience. It is this bank of experience which gives us our working rules of "right" and "wrong," and without them we could not but flounder. And it is these, constantly re-examined, which, in order to protect personality, have to be built into our codes of law, paradoxically, "without respect of persons." But love is the end of law precisely because it *does* respect persons—the unique, individual person—unconditionally. "The absoluteness of love is its power to go into the concrete situation, to discover what is demanded by the predicament of the concrete to which it turns." (HG, pp. 119–120.)

[9] *Ibid.*, pp. 8–9.

However, the melody to which this passage gives such fine expression cannot be played by itself. It belongs to a musical score in which there are other elements. There is, on the one hand, the centrality of the Christian community for the Christian ethic, and, for community life, law is essential and obligatory. Law is equally essential and obligatory for the life of the human community. On law depend those human and natural institutions, such as family, nation, state, etc., which as institutions need to be preserved for the good of man. And, finally, it must be clearly seen that love fulfills the law only as interior motive and exterior action are conjoined. The law is fulfilled when the law is obeyed for the reason of love. This is the argument of Paul when he says, "Love is the fulfilling of the law." (Rom. 13:10.) It is not enough simply not to covet or to commit adultery; these laws must be observed, and observed because one loves.

In our Lord's teaching on adultery or murder, for instance, he calls lust "adultery" and anger "murder," not because the intention is as bad as the deed, but because the law not to commit adultery and not to kill is not really observed when the obligations of love are denied through lust or anger. (Matt. 5:21–30.)

It is because the place of law in the Christian life is recognized that the New Testament writings are constantly concerned with the problems that obedience to the law raises. Obedience to the law must never tempt men to depend on their obedience for their salvation; it must never be allowed to become a substitute for the actual obligation to love; it must never be used either to condemn or justify, for it does not of itself prescribe what one must do; it must not determine the limits of men's enfranchisement in the gospel.

A consideration of these five negatives will serve to show why the New Testament takes the law more seriously than Bishop Robinson will allow. It can be stated

straightaway that the concern of the New Testament for
the law is not a concern for a prescriptive ethic. It is, as
we have said earlier, the result of recognizing the nature
of community both Christian and human.

1. When, therefore, it is insisted that salvation—
wholeness of life and acceptance by God—is by grace
alone through faith, at its deepest level this insistence is
grounded on the recognition that Christian obedience has
to be concrete and therefore must of necessity partake in
the predicament of man's sinfulness.

> When a man takes guilt upon himself in responsibility,
> and no responsible man can avoid this, he imputes this
> guilt to himself and to no one else; he answers for it; he
> accepts responsibility for it. He does not do this in the
> insolent presumptuousness of his own power, but he
> does it in the knowledge that this liberty is forced upon
> him and that in this liberty he is dependent on grace.
> Before other men the man of free responsibility is jus-
> tified by necessity; before himself he is acquitted by his
> conscience; but before God he hopes only for mercy.[10]

2. When it is insisted that obedience to the law cannot become a substitute for the obligation to love, at its
deepest level this insistence is grounded on the recognition that "the good" is not a deed that is done or a motive
that is entertained. The good is the very presence of Jesus
Christ in a specific situation and our share in that presence. The good is the whole.

> The good demands the whole, not only the whole of a
> man's outlook but his whole work, the whole man, to-
> gether with the fellow-men who are given to him. What
> sense would it have if only a part were to be called
> good, a motive perhaps, while the action is bad, or if
> the reverse were the case? Man is an indivisible whole,
> not only as an individual in his person and work but
> also as a member of the community of men and crea-

10 *Ibid.*, p. 216.

tures in which he stands. This indivisible whole, this reality which is founded on God and apprehended in Him, is what the question of good has in view.[11]

3. When it is insisted that by the law no man is condemned or justified, at its deepest level this insistence is grounded on the recognition that beyond the law is Jesus Christ, who is the judge. I am not guiltless because my conscience does not accuse me. I am not guilty when others condemn me. I am not acquitted when others uphold me. I am simply the Lord's. "But with me it is a very small thing that I should be judged by you or by any human court. I do not even judge myself." (I Cor. 4:3.)

4. When it is insisted that the law by itself does not prescribe what one must do, at its deepest level this insistence is grounded on the recognition that the content of obedience is distinct from the form of the law. The Western text of Luke 6:4 gives the following saying of our Lord's: "Blessed art thou if thou knowest what thou doest; but if thou knowest it not, then art thou accursed and a transgressor of the law." The law remains, even when the act performed is outside the law. Disobedience is responsible disobedience, and often one expression of this sense of responsibility is the willingness to accept the punishment decreed for one's disobedience. The problem here is simply that of openness to the world. As Oldham puts it:

> If Christianity is to become a living force it must break through the moulds in which it has become confined. It must recognize that what the Church offers to men is, because of its inescapable finitude as a human group, never the Christian revelation in its purity and fulness but only as much of that revelation as the natural capacities of its members and the cultural and sociological conditions of the period allow it to apprehend. You can-

11 *Ibid.*, pp. 59–60.

not put more into a pint pot than it will hold. For this reason the Church is always in need of the world.[12]

5. And lastly, when it is insisted that the law must not determine the limits of men's enfranchisement in the gospel, at its deepest level this insistence is grounded on the recognition that law is entangled in that which is historically contingent and that, therefore, there must be genuine willingness to follow where faithful response to the gospel leads. The controversy over the rite of circumcision in the early church affords a good example of this problem.

> The Pauline admonition against legalism: "Stand fast therefore in the liberty wherewith Christ hath made us free, and be not entangled again in the yoke of bondage," is inspired not merely by a consideration of the moral defects in any specific system of law but by the limits of law as such. The admonition has been shockingly disregarded by every version of the Christian faith. Each has found some way of making law, whether derived from Scripture or from the supposed absolutes of reason, too binding. The only exception to this legalism is found in modern sentimental forms of Christianity which assume that the supremacy of the law of love makes it possible to dispense with subordinate laws of justice. It is not possible to dispense with them; but it is important to recognize the historically contingent elements in every formulation of the principles of justice.[13]

This rather inadequate excursus into the issues concerning the law as they are discussed in the New Testament was undertaken for one purpose only—to show that the law has its own function, and that, while the questions that are raised concerning it in the New Testament are constantly borne in mind, it will not do to forget that

[12] Oldham, *op. cit.*, p. 88.
[13] Niebuhr, *Faith and History*, p. 221.

the law is as much part of the human situation as grace and that therefore there is no other foothold for the Christian in this dialectic except the foothold of faith in Christ, in whom a specific provision of the law is sometimes abrogated, but in whom the law itself is always fulfilled, and in whom grace becomes power to obey the possibilities of love.[14]

[14] I had written this chapter before I came across the book by Werner and Lotte Pelz entitled *God Is No More* (Victor Gollancz, Ltd., London, 1963). Here is an exposition of the Christian ethic that is really exciting. The words of Jesus live for the Christian; they beckon him to ever new possibilities, and, at the same time, promise them to him. The words of Jesus become the Way—they do not imprison.

7

"Thou Art My God"

THE CHRISTIAN LIFE is the life of a person who has died because of Jesus Christ and who lives because of Jesus Christ. Every situation in which the Christian ethic has to be incarnated is a situation in which Jesus Christ is intimately involved. The life he lives in that situation is the life that we must live with him. He is life. "For we are his workmanship, created in Christ Jesus for good works, which God prepared beforehand, that we should walk in them." (Eph. 2:10.)

If this is true, then there is only one resource for Christian living—it is that we remain dead: dead through our Baptism by which all claims upon us are dissolved and we belong to Christ alone (Rom. 6:4; II Cor. 5:14–17), and constantly dying as in partaking of the communion of his body and blood we become evidence and witnesses of his death before the world (I Cor. 11:26; II Cor. 6:9). It is about this one resource that we speak when we speak about worship and prayer.

Bishop Robinson, in his chapter on worship, seeks to answer Bonhoeffer's question: What is the place of worship and prayer in an entire absence of religion? And the answer he delineates is this:

> The purpose of worship is not to retire from the secular into the department of the religious, let alone to escape from "this world" into "the other world," but to open

oneself to the meeting of the Christ in the common, to that which has the power to penetrate its superficiality and redeem it from its alienation. (HG, p. 87.)

This is the essence of the religious perversion, when worship becomes a realm into which to withdraw from the world to "be with God"—even if it is only in order to receive strength to go back into it. . . . Worship, liturgy, on this understanding, is not meeting the holy *in* the common. (HG, pp. 86–87.)

In other words "the absence of religion" is taken to mean "presence in the world with God." The thrust of Bonhoeffer's question, on the other hand, seems to me to lie at another point. The essence of religion is "God for man." Its vulgarity is exposed in the *Deus ex machina* mentality that Bonhoeffer constantly castigates. So that the absence of religion is that position and posture in which "man for God" is the determinant.

No man [says Bonhoeffer] can look with undivided vision at God and at the world of reality so long as God and the world are torn asunder. Try as he may, he can only let his eyes wander distractedly from one to the other. But there is a place at which God and the cosmic reality are reconciled, a place at which God and man have become one. That and that alone is what enables man to set his eyes upon God and upon the world at the same time. This place does not lie somewhere out beyond reality in the realm of ideas. It lies in the midst of history as a divine miracle. It lies in Jesus Christ, the Reconciler of the world.[1]

It is this vision of God and the world at the same time in Jesus Christ which is the purpose and practice of worship. In such worship, the worshiper is lifted out of himself to the contemplation of God and finds there an uplifted hand pointing to the world to which the wor-

[1] Bonhoeffer, *Ethics,* p. 8.

shiper belongs as servant of his Master. (Isa. 6:8.) Worship is the true expression of man's creatureliness.

> The function of worship [says Bishop Robinson] is to make us more sensitive to these depths; to focus, sharpen and deepen our response to the world and to other people beyond the point of proximate concern (of liking, self-interest, limited commitment, etc.) to that of ultimate concern; to purify and correct our loves in the light of Christ's love; and in him to find the grace and power to be the reconciled and reconciling community. (HG, pp. 87–88.)

What the Bishop is talking about here are the consequences of true worship; the function of worship, however, is to establish man in his creatureliness before God his Creator, his Savior and Judge. This is why true worship is not religious either in motivation or in orientation. In it man stands God-directed and not world-directed, confronting God as He points to the world.

> I saw the Lord. . . . I said: "Woe is me!" . . . He touched my mouth. . . . I heard the voice of the Lord. . . . "Who will go for us?" . . . "Send me." (Isa., ch. 6.)

If this is what worship is, then it is quite clear what withdrawal for worship must be. What we actually go to church to do is not to find God as if he cannot be found elsewhere, but to enter into a relationship with him which is not possible apart from specific acts of worship. (HG, p. 90.) In worship and worship alone, in the church with the household of faith, do I experience in depth my embeddedness in the form of the church, the form in which the Christian faith exists. Says Barth:

> One can be a good citizen without belonging to a political party. One can be musical without joining a choral society. One can be a philosopher and as an eclectic or sceptic stand aloof from all philosophical movements, and the great philosophers are always above these. But

one cannot hold the Christian faith without holding it
in the church and with the church. The church is
neither a party nor a society nor a movement. *She is
the form in which the Christian faith exists,* because it
is faith in the One who died and rose again for the
many. Such a content must have and can only have
this form.[2]

In worship and worship alone to which I have withdrawn, not from the world, but from my own involvement in the world—as sinner, as witness and as servant
—do I glimpse the beauty which is his beauty even in the
common. The problem for most men is not that they have
no "vision of the sacredness of the secular" (HG, p. 90)
but that they have no vision of the sacredness of the
sacred.

> There is no sense [says Bishop Robinson] in which a
> Christian *has* to turn aside from the world in order to
> meet God—any more than the holy of holies is for
> him in the sanctuary. But there is a sense in which he
> *has* to go into the world, in unconditional love, in order
> to meet God; for "God is love" and "he who does not
> love does not know God." (HG, p. 100.)

The Bishop is profoundly wrong. There is a sense in
which a Christian has to turn aside from the world in
order to meet God: the simple sense in which he has to
turn aside from himself, even himself in all his activity
of loving. The holy is conveyed in the common but never
safely so unless it is already known in the holy. Brother
Lawrence claimed that he enjoyed the presence of God
as much in the kitchen as at the Mass. But he knew the
difference between them. My wife is *always* to me a
vision of loveliness, but that is because I have *often* seen
her in her beauty.

Also, in worship and in worship alone to which I have
withdrawn do I truly receive or renew my commission.

[2] Barth, *The Knowledge of God and the Service of God,* p. 155.

Bishop Robinson asks the question that Bonhoeffer asks, How can Jesus become the Lord even of those with no religion? And the answer which he gives is that all men have religion because all have knowledge of God, if God be the depth of man's being, man's experience of ultimate concern, man's ground of acceptance, and man's experience of being pulled short by that which is unconditional.

But Bonhoeffer's question is a question about Jesus, and the way back to theism for man in our time may not be the way back to Jesus at all. When Tillich says: "Religion is not a special function of man's spiritual life, but it is the dimension of depth in all of its functions," he is truly defining religion; but religion, by this definition, can be profoundly at variance with the mind of Christ. Jesus becomes Lord even of those with no religion either when he is accepted as Lord and there is no attempt by his servants to use him,[3] or when those who do not accept him are, nevertheless, included in the mission that he establishes.

Bonhoeffer, in his distinction between what he calls the penultimate and the ultimate, makes clear the nature of Christ's commission. He says:

> To give bread to the hungry man is not the same as to proclaim the grace of God and justification to him, and to have received bread is not the same as to have faith. Yet for him who does these things for the sake of the

[3] In his essay in *Soundings,* p. 89, H. A. Williams gives a pungent example of what the attitude "God for man" can mean. He says: "The practice of religion can be a form of lust. . . . First of all, I make an idol which I call Jesus of Nazareth or the Ascended Lord. Then I try to give myself value by identifying myself with the idol I have made. When the living me at times bursts through, and I become more than my own idol, I consider that I have sinned. When Swinburne wrote—'Thou hast conquered, O pale Galilean; the world has grown grey from thy breath,' he was describing lust masquerading as Christianity."

ultimate, and in the knowledge of the ultimate, this penultimate does bear a relation to the ultimate. It is a penultimate. The coming of grace is the ultimate. But we must speak of the preparing of the way, of the penultimate, the things before the last, for the sake of those who with their radicalism, which repudiates the things before the last, have encountered only failure, and who are now in danger of being thrown back even before the things before the last, and for the sake of those who stick fast in the things before the last and are content to remain there, but who must nevertheless now be claimed for the last things.[4]

It is in worship to which we have withdrawn from our works that we receive again our true commission, to prepare the way of the Lord even though "grace must in the end itself prepare and make level its own way and grace alone must ever anew render possible the impossible."[5]

We have spoken so far of three ways in which worship demands withdrawal—withdrawal from our singleness, withdrawal from our selves, withdrawal from our works. It is impossible, in speaking of worship, not to mention also that the world in which we worship and into which we withdraw is a larger world than this world whose boundary is death. "Therefore, with angels and archangels and all the company of heaven, we worship and adore Thy glorious Name."

Bishop Robinson's protest against thinking of God as "out there" is all right as far as it goes, but somehow it seems natural at least to think of the dead as "out there" in a life beyond death and as being with God in that life.

What happens in worship? God acts and man liturgizes, he serves God in His action. Man is for God. Worship begins at the point of Holy Baptism. They who are his worship him. "Know that the Lord is God! It is he that

[4] Bonhoeffer, *Ethics*, p. 95.
[5] *Ibid.*, p. 94.

made us, and we are his; we are his people, and the sheep of his pasture." (Ps. 100:3.) Worship ends at the point of Holy Communion. They who are nourished by him serve him.

And between these two points God speaks and man listens. By God's Word the heart is established in thankfulness; the soul is cleansed from sin and forgiven; the creature is refreshed at the hands of his Creator; the child enjoys himself in the presence of the Father and receives His promises; and the servant receives from his Lord the tasks that he must perform.

It is on worship, then, as the work of God, that emphasis must fall, an emphasis that points to that posture of man—man for God—which is his true posture in his New Being. Because he is man for God, he must listen to God's Word; he must also make his response of faith the true content of worship. As Barth puts it:

> It is because the church hears the Word of God and must hear it again that she preaches, baptises, observes the Lord's Supper and offers thanks. It is as the assembly of those who have heard God's Word and must hear it again that she meets. It is by listening to God that she serves Him. And it is by listening together to God that her members serve one another, as of course they must do. It is by hearing God that the church is built up, lives, grows, works and glorifies God's name in her own midst and in the world. She is the true church in proportion as she is the listening church. Any other goal which she may set herself in general or in detail may bear another name, but can only mean ultimately that the Word of God must be heard. Whatever goes beyond this hearing of God's Word, rests in God's good hands and is His work, not ours. But we have this piece of work to do—this is the thing which must be worked for and worked at in the church—the hearing of God's Word.[6]

[6] Barth, *The Knowledge of God and the Service of God*, p. 210.

The church service would be a lost cause if its content
were Christian piety and morality and not Christian
faith. But the church service is the most important,
momentous and majestic thing which can possibly take
place on earth, because its primary content is not the
work of man but the work of the Holy Spirit and con-
sequently the work of faith.[7]

Here we may make the transition from a discussion of
public worship to a discussion of private prayer, for the
content of private prayer, too, is the content of faith.
Bishop Robinson questions that attitude to private prayer
which considers it as a turning aside from the business of
the world to be with God. He would like to think of it as
penetration through the world to God. Prayer is an essential part of man's engagement with the world, and not
simply something that belongs to periods of disengagement. It will be illuminating to note the similarity and
the difference between this position and that set out in
the following quotation from George Goyder:

For me both prayer and work are subjective words.
They are what I think them to be from day to day and
make of them in practice. It so happens that I have
gradually become aware of the fact that neither prayer
nor work are what I used to think them. It is awkward,
but these words have taken it upon themselves to reverse their order, prayer becoming work and work shad-
ing into prayer. Or is it that work and prayer have
become so interpenetrated that the distinction between
them no longer matters? In both work and prayer the
reward of going out of oneself is to enable others to
enter one: . . . for do not other people speak to us
when we pray, as well as when we work rightly?[8]

I would like to approach the emphasis which I want to
make with an illustration from a conversation that I had

[7] *Ibid.*, p. 198.

[8] George Goyder in an essay in *Frontier,* Summer, 1963,
pp. 141–142.

with my father. We were speaking together on how to wait for and to receive God's guidance. He said to me: "Let me tell you what I do. When I am faced with any problem, I first gather all the facts about it that I can possibly get hold of. I also search my own heart to see what actual motives are operating in me as I seek a solution of the problem. I place these motives before God's judgment. Then I let the problem drift for a while, praying over it and about it. Little by little I see the possible alternative courses which I can pursue—true courses: and then I can sort of see my mind making itself up. I have decided. But when I have decided, I still wait, and if there is still a feeling of unrest I do not act. I must go on thinking, praying, deciding, until there is peace."

The issue, it has always seemed to me, is not between engagement and disengagement, between withdrawal from the world to observe periods of prayer and involvement in the world with God; rather, it is between the two attitudes of activity and passivity toward God. When my father said, "I let the problem drift," or when he said, "until there is peace," he was speaking of that attitude of passivity in which the child lives without anxiety because it knows that God loves and cares and rules. This is faith in the faithfulness of God. The child can be active in doing even when it is passive. This passivity toward God is the attitude of faith.

> God's claim to Lordship [says Barth] is put forward possessing the power to achieve its end.[9]
>
> God's commandment, revealed in Jesus Christ, [says Bonhoeffer] is always concrete speech to somebody. It is never abstract speech about something or about somebody. It is always an address, a claim, and it is so comprehensive and at the same time so definite that it leaves no freedom for interpretation or application, but only the freedom to obey or to disobey.[10]

[9] Barth, *The Knowledge of God and the Service of God*, p. 23.
[10] Bonhoeffer, *Ethics*, p. 246.

In other words, at the heart of private prayer is this experience of being at rest in God in Christ: and it does not matter whether such prayer is the set of the soul in the midst of work or its priceless possession in moments of withdrawal. In this connection there seems to me to be real illumination in these words of H. A. Williams:

> St. Paul and St. John continue the attacks made by Jesus upon the restless, scheming, anxious pretensions of the conscious self. Justification by faith means that a man has nothing else on which to depend except his receptivity to what he can never own or manage. . . . However Christians may have used their Christianity there is abundant evidence in the New Testament that the Christian Gospel, far from boosting the pretensions of the known and controllable self, seeks its subservience to a trustful confidence in a God who is creating what I am by means of which I am unaware.[11]

I must admit that when Bishop Robinson speaks of himself and his problems in the practice of prayer, he speaks also for me. My problems are almost identical with his. But I cannot say with him, "The pentecostal point is in the engagement." For me the pentecostal point is when I cease to struggle, whether in prayer or in service, and "go to sleep."

> The kingdom of God is as if a man should scatter seed upon the ground, and should sleep and rise night and day, and the seed should sprout and grow, he knows not how. (Mark 4:26–27.)

> For so he giveth his beloved sleep. (Ps. 127:2, KJV.)

> God's gifts come to his loved ones, as they sleep. (Ps. 127:2, Moffatt's translation.)

And it is precisely because this is so, that it is wise to maintain both the prayer-dimension of work as well as the work-dimension of prayer. Prayer is also something that

[11] Williams, quoted by A. R. Vidler, ed., in *Soundings*, pp. 94–95.

one must do. Why cannot it be that there are stated times each day for prayer—times that are *chronoi*—when one prays as a habit and as a routine, be the time spent long or short, or very short? And why cannot it be that each day there are also extended periods of prayer—periods that are *kairoi*—when work and witness spill over into prayer and there is unhurried waiting upon God? And why cannot work and prayer be joined by acts of ejaculatory prayer that make work an expression of thankfulness to God and make prayer the offering of our work?

When you give alms, said Jesus, hide the fact. Let your charity be a secret. And your Father, who sees what is secret, will reward you. When you pray, he said, go into your own room, shut your door, and pray to your Father privately, your Father who is your secret. Also, when you fast, let it be a secret between you and your Father. And your Father, who knows all secrets, will reward you. "I keep it a secret." "He is my secret." "Only he is in the secret." (Matt. 6:2–18.) There is no better description of one's personal life in relation to God. Nor is there a sharper warning concerning one's personal relation to the institutions of religion than is contained in our Lord's words, "The sabbath was made for man, not man for the sabbath" (Mark 2:27). The important thing is not that the Sabbath should be observed, but that the observance of the Sabbath should be integral to man's worship and service of God. The issue is simply and only that God alone should be worshiped, and that everything else should subserve this purpose. The issue is also that men must worship him.

In the words of the psalmist: "Thou art my God. . . . Thou alone art God." (Ps. 86:2, 10.)

Epilogue

I HAVE FINISHED the book that I set out to write. It has been a rewarding experience to wrestle with the "obstinate questions" raised by Bishop Robinson and to discuss the answers that he has sought to give. I have suggested that the Biblical message itself demands a more radical recasting of the ways in which the Christian faith is often presented to the men of our time, a recasting more radical than even their questions demand. For the task of Christian preaching and teaching is to allow the questions that God asks of men to be heard and to help them to understand and to answer. The answers lie inevitably at the point where this hearing actually takes place.

I now append as an epilogue to this book a direct statement such as I would make to the kind of person whom I have had in mind all the time. It says what essentially the Christian faith makes me say when I reflect upon it. God's declaration, "I am God almighty," is for the Christian both the beginning and the ending of all that he believes, of all that he hopes for, and of all that by which he is sustained. It may be that, with all its inadequacies, this epilogue will convey what in the book itself must have been a muffled note because the book was by its very nature controversial. It is unashamedly couched in the language of the Bible because of my conviction that this language is not all that opaque and that he who does listen to it truly hears.

> Christ! I am Christ's! and let the name suffice you,
> Ay, for me too He greatly hath sufficed;
> Lo with no winning words I would entice you,
> I have no honour and no friend but Christ.

> Yes thro' life, death, thro' sorrow and thro' sinning
> He shall suffice me, for He hath sufficed:
> Christ is the end, for Christ was the beginning,
> Christ the beginning, for the end is Christ.[1]

In the great cathedrals of Russia, indeed in practically all the churches of Eastern Orthodoxy everywhere, the figure of the Pantocrator is dominant. One looks up at the dome, and the face of the Pantocrator is seen looking down. The Almighty, he who at the last will prevail, whose strength is sufficient for the accomplishment of his will—he it is to whom our churches bear witness. Always, as the waves beat upon the shores of the sea, there comes, beating upon the affirmations of this world, the shout of heaven: "Hallelujah. For the Lord our God the Almighty reigns" (Rev. 19:6).

The Biblical revelation places the declaration of God as God Almighty in the context of the story of Abraham. Abraham is an old man, seventy-five years of age, when God comes to him at Haran and calls him to become the father of a people. Twenty-five years pass and yet Abraham has no son. How is God's promise to be fulfilled? Abraham is now ninety-nine years old, so that, even if twenty-five years ago there was a human possibility to meet the divine promise, there is none now. If God's word is to be fulfilled, God alone will have to fulfill it. Will he? He says he will.

In the New Testament, the word "Pantocrator" occurs eight times in the book of The Revelation. In the rest of

[1] "Saint Paul," by F. W. H. Myers (verse 1, line 4, "Paul has" has been altered to "I have").

the New Testament, however, it occurs only once. It comes in Paul's second letter to the Corinthians where, when quoting a series of passages from the Old Testament, Paul underlines the same truth that is found in the story of Abraham. "And I will be a father to you, and you shall be my sons and daughters, says the Lord Almighty." (II Cor. 6:18.) It was grace that gave us birth into the family of God.

The context in which Paul strikes this note concerning God's Almightiness is a discussion about marriage between believer and unbeliever. "Can there be a compact," he asks, "between the temple of God and the idols of the heathen? And the temple of the living God is what we are." (II Cor. 6:16, NEB.) God alone is sufficient for the fulfillment of God's purposes, and they who believe in him must refuse aid from that which is not God. He who would serve God will have to serve God alone, and he who waits for the fulfillment of God's purposes must learn to wait until that situation arrives when God has made it clear that it is his purposes which are being fulfilled, and that it is he who is fulfilling them. Entangling alliances, whether of method or of goal, simply delay and compromise that fulfillment.

In 1951 there was a pilgrimage to Washington organized by American churchmen. On that occasion, September 28, the Right Reverend Angus Dun, then Protestant Episcopal Bishop of the Diocese of Washington, preached the sermon. In it he said: "The God who makes himself known to us in Scripture, who makes himself known to us in Christ, cannot be bargained with, cannot be mobilized or used for human purposes—he can only be trusted and loved and served. There are frightened servants of Mammon who think this might be a good time to finance the church to fight communism and its godlessness so that Mammon might be served in peace. On the surface there is considerable appeal in the idea that the churches might be mobilized to strengthen the weak political sinews of the traditionally Christian West. But you who come here in the spirit of pilgrimage surely know that Christian faith and devotion cannot be financed from outside, nor at bottom can Christian faith and devotion be mobilized by political leadership for political end, however good."

In all Christian worship, in every Christian enterprise, in meeting with faith the problems of our time, there is one thing of basic importance. It is to remember, as Paul reminds us, who we are. We are sons and daughters of God as the result of God's action alone. Isaac is always only God's possibility. We were "not born of any human stock, or by the fleshly desire of a human father, but [are] the offspring of God himself" (John 1:13–14, NEB). In the words of James, "Of his set purpose, by declaring the truth, he gave us birth" (James 1:18, NEB).

In the book of The Revelation, the affirmation of God as Pantocrator is invariably made in association with the concept of God as controlling the march of time. He is and was and is to come. He fills time with his judgments. Time is the chronicle of his mighty deeds. His Kingdom is time's fulfillment.[2] Here is the kind of faith for our time, not that we believe in it because it is relevant, but that it is relevant because it is true. In *A Sleep of Prisoners*, Christopher Fry makes a voice from the Furnace speak these words:

> The frozen misery
> Of centuries breaks, cracks, begins to move;
> The thunder is the thunder of the floes,
> The thaw, the flood, the upstart Spring.
> Thank God our time is now when wrong
> Comes up to face us everywhere,
> Never to leave us till we take
> The longest stride of soul men ever took.

[2] Rev. 1:8; 4:8; 11:17; 15:3; 16:7, 14; 19:6, 15; 21:22.

Affairs are now soul size,
The enterprise
Is exploration into God.[3]

When we allow this word "Pantocrator" to speak to us, what does it say? When we explore it, what do we find?

We find, in the first instance, that it encompasses all time with the mercy and majesty of God. He who holds all time in his hand is, to use the Biblical image, "the Lamb that was slain, predestined before the foundation of the world" (I Peter 1:19, NEB, and Rev. 13:8, NEB). Jesus died because he loved and because he insisted on loving even when his love was rejected. The cross is the only thing men can do to a love they do not want when it will not let them go. This love and its cross are the very foundations of the world. They were there from the beginning, they will be there until the end. He who is Almighty, should he love, will suffer. The majesty of God is the splendor of that love poured out—"Immortal Love, forever full, Forever flowing free, Forever shared, forever whole, A never ebbing sea!"

I want to remember this when I suffer, because when I suffer for the reason that I love, I know that I am being accorded the privilege of sharing in his cross. "Can you drink?" Jesus asked James and John. " 'Can you drink the cup that I am to drink?' 'We can,' they replied. Then he said to them, 'You shall.' " (Matt. 20:22–23, NEB.) But I want to remember his cross, not only when I have to carry it, but also when others have to carry it because of me. It is then that I know unmistakably that I am held within his love.

Not only is all time encompassed by him who is Almighty, but every moment of time comes as a gift from

[3] Christopher Fry, *A Sleep of Prisoners: A Play* (Oxford University Press, 1951), p. 209. Reprinted with the permission of the publisher.

him. The singers of Israel knew little about the fullness
of life beyond death, so that they saw more clearly the
meaning of this life on earth. Every new day meant for
them a sign of the forgiveness of God, a renewed call to
repentance and faith. "This is the day which the Lord has
made; let us rejoice and be glad in it." (Ps. 118:24.)
Every day is God's gift. Every day is auspicious with
God's love. Astrologers, with their predictions of good
days and bad days, might have plausibility if it were true
that God could forget me and leave me to the mercy of
buffeting circumstances! But does he forget? "Can a
woman forget her sucking child? . . . Yet I will not forget
you." (Isa. 49:15.)

It is true that "Pantocrator" is a word that sweeps the
far horizons. But I have deliberately struck first the personal note because it is precisely here that weakness lies
in the lives of most men. The belief that God will finally
prevail over all things seems to come to most of us more
easily than the faith that in our own personal lives we
are already and always within his prevailing love and
power. And yet how natural this mood of doubt is, for,
in the last analysis, it is me and the wrongness within me
that I know best of all.

The words of Whittier in his poem "Andrew Rykman's
Prayer" express so well what most of us know.

> For myself alone I doubt;
> All is well, I know, without;
> I alone the beauty mar,
> I alone the music jar,
> Yet with hands by evil stained
> And an ear by discord pained,
> I am groping for the keys
> Of the heavenly harmonies.

But he who is Almighty not only holds all things in his
hands, he is also the beginning and the ending of all
things. Not only is it true that we shall not grope in vain,

it is also true that we need not grope at all. It is he who finds us. He begins the race that we run. Suddenly you find yourself with the baton in your hands. Who put it there? Perhaps your father, perhaps your mother; maybe your friend, your teacher, your pastor—but it was Jesus who ran the race they ran. It was he who caused you to be chosen as a member of this relay team. It is he who tells you: "Run and do not drop the baton. Your son is at the end of this lap waiting for it. The next generation in your country depend on your faithfulness now."

It is true enough that sometimes one gets tired, or weary, or despairing. One is tempted to say as Browning does in the poem "Paracelsus":

> I give the fight up: let there be an end,
> A privacy, an obscure nook for me,
> I want to be forgotten even by God.

But the temptation passes, and because faith is fixed in the almightiness of God, hope springs up again. Browning goes on to say:

> If I stoop into a dark tremendous sea of cloud,
> It is but for a time; I press God's lamp
> Close to my breast; its splendour, soon or late,
> Will pierce the gloom; I shall emerge one day.

So the race is run, without haste or hurry, but steadily and persistently. Yes, there will be obstacles on the way, obstacles that challenge faith and corrupt hope. But to believe in the Almighty is to remember that no obstacle will be too great to overcome or circumvent. "God keeps faith, and he will not allow you to be tested above your powers, but when the test comes he will at the same time provide a way out, by enabling you to sustain it." (I Cor. 10:13, NEB.) Until, at the last, the race is completed for each person by the Lord himself, as he will complete it for mankind as a whole. He began the race; he will finish it. He runs the last lap. (Heb. 12:2, NEB.)

But precisely because he is the beginning and the ending, it is his race that we run, it is in his service that we are engaged, it is his cause that we espouse. The proximate goals for which we contend must, therefore, never be allowed to occupy the center of our loyalty or to become the object of our worship. In what large measure has it become true that the divisions between Christians are the result of quarrels concerning secondary issues that have been allowed to occupy the center! In spite of many differences, it is only in the living of a common family life that we, as Christians, will finally recover the proportions of our faith. There is only one race—the race that he began and that we must run: the race concerning which he prayed that we may all be one that the world may believe that it was the Father who sent him. (John 17:21.) How will the world believe that Jesus is the "sent" of God, if that sending is represented in the world by a multiplicity of quarreling and competing causes?

There is still a third facet of this Biblical affirmation that God is almighty. His love encompasses the whole; his initiative begins, sustains, and completes the course of the life of man and of mankind; his will is the meaning of every moment. "From the foundation of the world," "the beginning and the ending"—that is Almighty God; he is also the "Now."

There are three instances in the Gospels where the immediate moment becomes, on the lips of Jesus, the moment of crisis. "Today you shall be with me in Paradise." (Luke 23:43, NEB.) "Zacchaeus, be quick and come down; I must come and stay with you today." (Luke 19:5, NEB.) "You fool, this very night you must surrender your life." (Luke 12:20, NEB.) It is no accident that in all these three cases, the divine moment has a judgment and a meaning contrary to that which earth has pronounced. The thief must die—No, he shall live. Zacchaeus is an outcast from society—No, I shall stay with him. The rich man is a success—No, he is a fool.

The discerning of the divine will and judgment in the given moment is the burden that is placed upon us by the almightiness of God. Here we cannot always walk without stumbling, but we shall learn as we walk. Only one thing is required—that we keep our souls sensitive to the stab of his word, and that we do not dull our minds with platitudes or dope them with clichés or be satisfied in our souls because our performance is average and our fellows approve. The poet Wordsworth, in "The Excursion" (Bk. 5), considers the religious world of his time:

> Who can reflect, unmoved upon the round
> Of smooth and solemnised complacencies,
> By which, in Christian lands, from age to age
> Profession mocks performance. Earth is sick,
> And heaven is weary, of the hollow words
> Which States and Kingdoms utter when they talk
> Of truth and justice, . . .
>
> A light of duty shines on every day
> For all; and yet how few are warmed or cheered.

Every day, at the given moment—it is then that obedience must be rendered to Almighty God.

What is the consequence for life of God's concern for the meaning of the moment? Whenever the devil seeks to lead us along a particular way, he shows us the distant scene. He took Jesus "to a very high mountain, and showed him all the kingdoms of the world in their glory" (Matt. 4:8, NEB). But when God seeks to guide us, he makes clear only the next step. We never know where God is taking us till he has taken us there. He insists that we accept the meaning of the moment. It is the devil who tempts us with visions of the future—"You will be like God," "You will have the kingdoms of the world" (Gen. 3:5; Matt. 4:9). In our earthly life we are so used to calculating consequences that we find it hard to learn the lesson of faith. But it is that lesson which we must learn. To choose the moment is to live by the Almightiness of God.

"I am God Almighty." "I am . . . who is and was and is to come." "I am the Alpha and the Omega." "But exhort one another every day, as long as it is called 'today'."[4]

[4] Gen. 17:1; Rev. 1:8; Heb. 3:13.